BENETTO

BENETTON

FORMULA 1 RACING TEAM

Alan Henry

Haynes Publishing

First published in November 1998

A catalogue record for this book is
available from the British Library

ISBN: 1 85960 424 2

Library of Congress catalog card no. 98-72319

Haynes North America Inc.,
861 Lawrence Drive, Newbury Park,
California 91320, USA.

Published by Haynes Publishing, Sparkford,
Nr Yeovil, Somerset BA22 7JJ, UK.

Tel: 01963 440635 Fax: 01963 440001
Int. tel: +44 1963 440635 Fax +44 1963 440001
E-mail: sales@haynes-manuals.co.uk
Web site: http://www.haynes.com

Designed and typeset by G&M, Raunds, Northamptonshire
Printed and bound in Great Britain by J. H. Haynes and Co. Ltd, Sparkford

Contents

Acknowledgements

I would particularly like to thank Benetton F1 Chief Executive David Richards for his help and accessibility in assisting with the task of producing this book. For other interviews I am grateful to Alexander Wurz, Giancarlo Fisichella, Pat Symonds and Joan Villadelprat, while Julia Horden, Andrea Ficarelli and Luca Mazzocco in the Benetton press office at Enstone worked well beyond the call of duty in helping to field a seemingly interminable succession of inquiries from the author. They all have my grateful thanks.

Alan Henry
Tillingham
August 1998

Introduction

Nothing can be taken for granted in the fast-moving, unpredictable world of Formula 1. Literally as this volume was being prepared for press, Benetton's Chief Executive David Richards resigned his post at the head of possibly the most colourful contemporary grand prix team in the business. It was a decision of seismic significance.

This technically accomplished F1 operation had since the glory years of 1994/5 often seemed to be bugged by the sort of intra-team pseudo-political controversy which had so often convulsed Ferrari down the decades. The appointment of Richards in October 1997 was regarded as a decision taken to steer the team into calmer, more considered waters. A rational, pragmatic and extremely seasoned motorsport entrepreneur, a former World Rally Champion co-driver, and the founder of Prodrive, one of the UK's most accomplished specialist performance engineering companies, Richards was seen as a safe pair of hands at a time when Benetton needed to consolidate its competitive position after a difficult couple of seasons. Not safe enough, it seems.

Richards, speaking in the run-up to the last race of the season, says he left after the Benetton family declined to endorse his long-term plan to restore their cars to front-running form. The family reckoned he was 'too radical'. However, Richards – whose rallying partnership with Subaru had delivered four World Championship crowns – quickly made it clear that he had learned a lot from his year in grand prix racing and certainly did not discount a return.

'My time with Benetton has left me with a clear idea of what the basic issues involved in F1 really are,' he said, 'and what organisational structures are required. For me, Ferrari is the only team which has sustainable value. Developing a brand image which is on a par with Ferrari is the challenge which other teams now have to get to grips with. I do not underestimate what any of the other teams have achieved over the years, but I believe the sport has now reached a watershed which will sort out who will be the most successful amongst the next generation of F1 teams. It was the timescale for change which the Benetton family did not feel able to go with. I wanted to see some very significant changes with virtually immediate effect and the board did not think they were necessary. But without the endorsement of my long-term plan, which was due to be implemented on 1 October (1998), I was not prepared to stay on.'

There was much speculation as to what Richards would do next. Many observers had him linked to Ford's F1 effort, perhaps in a management role with the struggling new Stewart team. Richards was not saying. 'I expect to be back in F1 in due course,' was all that he would admit. But if so, without having his hands tied. 'The key to my interest is actually to have the final say in the running of any operation in which I might become involved.'

At that stage Benetton was on course for one of its worst seasons for a decade. Yet there had been times during 1998 when the team seemed to be making solid progress towards recovering some of the momentum lost the previous two seasons. Indeed, there were a couple of occasions when one of its promising new young guns looked a possible candidate for a victory. The first such performance came in the most glamorous race of the year.

The scene was motor racing's jewel in the crown, the Monaco Grand Prix,

run through the streets of the fairy tale Principality which nestles on a thin strip of real estate between France and the balmy Mediterranean. As Mika Hakkinen's McLaren-Mercedes disappeared into the distance to win commandingly, young Italian hero Giancarlo Fisichella was left driving magnificently in second place at the wheel of his Benetton B198. For lap after lap, with absolute precision, Fisichella displayed enormous maturity as he refused to be intimidated by the presence in his mirrors of Ferrari ace Michael Schumacher, not a man to be patient when thwarted.

There was a nice symmetry about this. Earlier in his career, Schumacher had forged a reputation as Benetton's most successful driver. From the time he won his first race for the team in 1992, the focused German progressively established himself as one of the greatest drivers of his era. But now he was being shown the way by a bright-eyed new boy for whom Benetton would hold out similar hopes.

Fisichella survived to finish a superb second at Monaco while Schumacher made a rare error, colliding with the other Benetton driven by Alexander Wurz. The Italian driver would later follow that up with an equally impressive second place, this time behind Schumacher, in the Canadian Grand Prix, during which he led an F1 race for the first time in his brief career.

Benetton may not always have been the most successful team in F1 in terms of hard results, although Schumacher's World Championships certainly helped its batting average. However, it has always been newsworthy (sometimes

Preparing Fisichella's Benetton for the 1998 Monaco Grand Prix where after a superbly controlled race he finished second. (Formula One Pictures)

for controversies it might rather forget), energetic and overtly ambitious.

It is also perhaps no coincidence that, since the formation of Benetton Formula, the team's cars have been among the most colourful ever seen in this sport. The emphasis on colour, sometimes boldly contrasting, some- times subtly blended, has long been a Benetton hallmark and, come to that, was effectively responsible for the Group's very existence.

When Leone Benetton died in 1945, he left behind a wife and four children – Luciano, Giuliana, Gilberto and Carlo – in the town of Treviso in the foothills of the Italian Dolomites north of Venice. So soon after the end of the Second World War, this was a time of considerable privation, but the people

of Treviso had long been known for their resourcefulness in the face of adversity, so it was quite in keeping that the two eldest children wanted to leave school as quickly as possible in order to earn a living.

Aged 15, Luciano Benetton took a job in a men's clothing shop, while Giuliana was two years younger when she became a skein winder at one of the local knitwear companies. However, as a hobby Giuliana used to create brightly coloured sweaters for the family on a home knitting machine and, in 1955, Luciano deployed his growing entrepreneurial feel by putting a proposal to his sister. 'Why don't we leave our jobs, pool our resources and go into business on our own?' Giuliana agreed. The business began modestly.

Yet within a few years, thanks to Luciano's commercial skills, they needed a minibus to transport employees to the small workshop established near the Benetton family home.

Concentrating on selling to specialist knitwear shops rather than department stores ensured that their products gained more exposure in the market place. Then came a crucial breakthrough. Luciano attended the 1960 Olympic Games, held in Rome, and met a group of knitwear wholesalers who agreed to handle the Benetton lines. Sales blossomed.

David's ideas were too radical, too long-term

By 1965, after another five years of growth, the Benetton organisation was formally established with Luciano as Chief Executive, major shareholder and marketing strategist, Giuliana as chief designer, Gilberto in charge of financial matters and Carlo, the youngest of the four, responsible for production at the newly opened first Benetton factory at Ponzano, near Treviso. The subsequent expansion of the Benetton Group was so spectacular that it warranted a special study by the Harvard Business School. In a sense, a glamorous sport such as grand prix racing was tailor-made for the Benetton family's international marketing and promotional requirements.

The first Benetton sponsorship involvement was with the Tyrrell-Ford team in 1983, highlighted by Michele Alboreto's victory in the Detroit Grand Prix. Later that season there was a delightful coincidence which led the Tyrrell type 012 to carry identification from Benetton's 012 range designed for youngsters up to the age of 12. A clever coincidence? Or shrewd marketing? Nobody was quite certain.

Benetton switched to Alfa Romeo in 1984, but it was clear that the Italian marque was never really going to achieve the sustained levels of success which its sponsor was looking for. Consequently, the Italian knitwear company decided to hedge its bets in 1985 and invested heavily in the Toleman F1 team which it would eventually take over and rename. The following year Gerhard Berger posted the first Benetton grand prix victory in Mexico City. In 1987 the team began a technical partnership with Ford which would last eight seasons and deliver Schumacher's 1994 World Championship.

In the meantime, there would be much colour and spectacle surrounding the team's promotional and car launch activities which, even by the standards of the late 1980s, were extravagently staged.

As an example, for the 1988 Benetton-Ford launch, the international media assembled in London's docklands where they were given Benetton Formula boiler suits to wear. We soon realised why. Marooned in the centre of a dazzling, white-walled studio, we huddled together for protection as Benetton mechanics hurled multi-coloured swathes of paint up the walls around us. This done, there was a blinding flash and Thierry Boutsen's car came apparently accelerating through one of the walls before rolling to a stop in front of us, surrounded by smoking dry ice. In 1994 the theme was repeated at the Benetton factory where J.J. Lehto appeared through a paper barrier in similar theatrical style.

Finally, to top everyone else for sheer bravura, the 1996 Benetton-Renaults were unveiled in the fashionable Sicilian resort of Taormina, with Jean Alesi and Gerhard Berger driving the cars through the streets against a backdrop of ruined Roman temples and admiring locals. On the face of it, this was to celebrate the switch of Benetton's official entrants licence from Britain to Italy, but the team never needed much of an excuse for a major beano. Predictably, there was enormous international media coverage.

Publicity was meat and drink to Flavio Briatore, who had spearheaded Benetton's US retail operation before being appointed by the family to run the team in 1989.

Briatore cultivated the enigmatic image. With his deep tan, dark glasses and habit of chain smoking even on the pit wall, he was very much F1's mystery man. A regular item in the gossip columns romancing a succession of lovelies, this sleek member of the international glitterati admitted he knew little about F1 when he started in the business, but he was a quick learner with an eye to the sport's wider promotional value. 'Flav' became very much a character in his own right, always available to the press, always ready to share his views on the more daft anomalies thrown up by what can be a distinctly over-intense business.

What brought this all to an end is difficult to pinpoint. It may have been that the success achieved during his tenure imbued him with a dangerously independent streak which unsettled the Benetton family. Perhaps he just got tired. Either way, at the end of the 1997 season, Briatore stood down.

His successor could hardly have been more different in style, temperament and outlook. Towards the end of the 1998 season, David Richards seemed to be getting into his stride as the new Chief Executive and, having spent several months quietly watching the way F1 worked, began to stamp his own identity on the team. But the honeymoon period led to an abruptly unexpected divorce. The chalice now passed on to Rocco Benetton. Short-term anyway – early rumours suggested that Arrows boss Tom Walkinshaw might possibly return to the team he had helped lead to victory in 1994.

Youngest son of Luciano, the 29-year-old had joined the team that season as Richards' assistant, describing his role as helping to bridge the gap more effectively between the UK and Italian operations. Rocco, hardly a seasoned campaigner himself, now looked to have his work cut out, handling the fall-out from this painful parting, and rebuilding morale at Enstone, not least among the two young drivers who were known to enjoy a good relationship with Richards. Manfully he maintained that the new regime was probably best for everyone in the end. 'We had different strategies and plans,' he told *Autosport*. 'David's ideas were probably too radical, too pointed towards the long term.'

Benetton has always tried to nurture new talent. In 1991, Briatore and Walkinshaw, then Engineering Director, pulled out all the stops to secure the services of a young German driver who had made his F1 debut for Jordan in the Belgian GP. Michael Schumacher won his first two World Championships with Benetton, using Ford and Renault engines respectively, and quickly became established as the greatest driver of his generation.

The problem for Benetton of course came at the end of the 1995 season when the German moved to Ferrari. Having enjoyed the services of this outstanding performer, it was now diffi-cult to see how the situation could be sustained. The decision was taken to sign former Ferrari team-mates Gerhard Berger and Jean Alesi, but they were not in the same class.

It was perhaps inevitable that the Benetton workforce bridled somewhat when faced with these new drivers. They were, felt some, time-expired and past their best. It was a harsh judge-ment, particularly when one bears in mind Berger's dazzling German Grand Prix victory in 1997 and Alesi's consis-tent run of second places over the two seasons he was with the squad. Yet that was very thin milk by contrast with what had gone before. Consequently, it seemed a shrewd move to sign Giancarlo Fisichella and Alexander Wurz for the 1998 season.

These two youngsters were promis-ing, motivated and highly committed to the task. Despite some interest in Wurz subsequently shown by Ferrari, neither he nor Fisichella seemed set to be deflected from maturing to grand prix winning status with Benetton. Moreover, if it had not been for the performance drop-off displayed by Bridgestone tyres in the second half of 1998 – or the improvement from the rival Goodyears, whichever way you look at it – the chances are that Fisichella and Wurz would have consolidated their early season achievements. Which would have pleased everyone.

In 1998 the Benetton team had a portfolio of sponsors every bit as cosmopolitan as the team's original founding company. Whilst wholly owning the operation, the team also continued to carry its 'United Colors of Benetton' badging as a subsidiary spoonsor alongside Japan Tobacco's Mild Seven cigarette brand which is the team's official title sponsor. These sponsors were further supplemented by Playlife, a multi-national sports equip-ment manufacturing group consisting of Nordica, Prince, Kastle, Rollerblade, Asolo, Langert, Ekterlon, Killerloop and Nitro.

There was also Federal Express, the world's largest express transportation company; Korean Air, one of the ten largest airlines in the world which flies to 78 cities in 34 countries; Akai, the worldwide leader in the electronics industry; Bridgestone, the world's largest tyre supplier; Hewlett Packard (computers), D2 Privat (telecom), PI.SA (ceramic tiles), Rach (fruit juices and sports drinks), Minichamps (scale models) and OMB (household refuse disposal equipment).

This wide-ranging support contributed the estimated £45 million needed to run the team in 1998, a figure which included £13 million lease fees to Renault's affiliated company, Mecachrome, for the reliable and rugged V10 engines.Mecachrome was transmuted into a new company, Supertec, for 1999, ironically under the management of Flavio Briatore. All customers were expected to have to pay a 15 per cent price rise under the new deal which would push Benetton's engine bill to around £16 million.

In the longer-term it was difficult to see how the team could consolidate its position without a factory-provided engine – and the development programme which goes with such a deal. The whole ethos of contemporary grand prix racing has proved, time and again, that a team needs an exclusive partnership with a totally committed major manufacturer in order to sustain the momentum of a march to the front of the field.

When David Richards headed the team, many F1 insiders believed that this hurdle would eventually be cleared by a works deal with Ford, picking up the threads of a relationship which culminated with Schumacher's 1994 title. Richards' company Prodrive had just concluded a deal to prepare the works Ford Mondeos in the 1999 British Touring Car Championship, an alliance which raised speculation about a possible new Benetton-Ford F1 partnership. That now seemed unlikely to develop any further.

At the season's finale in Japan, the B198s were again well off the pace, with both Giancarlo and Alex complaining of poor balance and lack of grip throughout practice and qualify-

Refuelling staff and guests is a vital part of a grand prix. (Formula One Pictures)

United we stand? Chief Executive Rocco Benetton with his two young drivers, Giancarlo Fisichella (left) and Alexander Wurz. (Formula One Pictures)

ing. They finished the race eighth and ninth respectively. Benetton ended a disappointing fifth in the Constructors' title, small beer on the face of it perhaps, but deeply significant from the standpoint of morale.

Rocco Benetton, making his first appearance as Chief Executive, confirmed that he would do his utmost to secure Renault works engines in the near future if the French car maker decided on a return to F1. 'The team needs an engine manufacturer as a partner who shares our targets.'

Over the winter Benetton would be working hard to knit the pieces together again into a united push for progress in 1999.

NOTE: David Richards' resignation came as this book was going to press. The publishers decided that the chapters should remain as written, with Richards quoted as the boss, describing his hopes for the team, his admiration for its young drivers, and his plans for moulding a new culture in which Benetton would have a real chance of returning to the glory years. It is a testament to what might have been.

Chapter 1

The

early years

Benetton's Formula 1 success has its roots in the audacious pioneering efforts of the Toleman team which began contesting the World Championship in 1981 with its own specially commissioned four-cylinder turbocharged engine developed by Brian Hart.

Early days. Derek Warwick in the Toleman-Hart TG181 before practice for the team's F1 debut, the 1981 San Marino GP. Both his and team-mate Brian Henton's cars failed to qualify. (Formula One Pictures)

The Toleman Group car delivery firm had been founded in 1926 by Albert Toleman and became involved in motorsport sponsorship in 1969 when it supported a club racing Ford Escort driven by amateur racer Colin Hawker. The driving force behind Toleman's motor racing activities was Alex Hawkridge who joined the company in 1968 and quickly worked his way through the ranks to become the Group's Managing Director.

As a result of their club racing involvement, Hawkridge quickly became aware of the commercial potential offered by motorsport sponsorship. By the late 1970s Toleman was contesting the European Formula 2 Championship and in 1980 Brian Henton dominated this prestige second division series with the team's own bespoke Toleman-Hart TG280s which were designed by Rory Byrne, later to become Chief Designer of the Benetton F1 operation.

Next step, the bigtime. Hawkridge cajoled Brian Hart into developing the 1.5-litre four-cylinder turbo F1 engine in time for the 1981 San Marino Grand Prix. Brian reckoned he needed longer to ready the programme, but Hawkridge was insistent. The early 1980s was politically a highly volatile period for F1 development and Alex believed it was necessary to get a foot in the door as quickly as possible. If Toleman passed up the opportunity, he reasoned, they might miss the grand prix boat altogether.

Henton struggling with the unwieldy TG181 in practice for the 1981 Austrian GP.
(Formula One Pictures)

The first Toleman-Hart TG181 was simply uncompetitive. The team – at that stage sponsored by Candy, the Italian domestic appliances people – spent much of the 1981 season carrying out its development programme during race weekends, much to the frustration

of drivers Henton and Derek Warwick. Not until the third last race of the season, the Italian Grand Prix at Monza, did Henton manage to qualify for the first time, although he did complete the distance, albeit three laps behind. Warwick had to wait for his F1 debut until the season's finale at Las Vegas. His race ended in retirement – gearbox trouble.

Yet prospects began to look brighter. Throttle response – a huge challenge to surmount with the first generation turbocharged engines – was gradually

improved and, although Warwick and his new team-mate Teo Fabi, struggled through 1982 with a revised version of the TG181, a totally new carbon-fibre composite challenger was developed by Byrne shortly before the end of the season.

Unfortunately for the Toleman design team, the F1 technical regulations for 1983 were changed dramatically, almost at the last minute. Byrne had to re-work the car to conform with the new flat-bottom chassis rules and the resultant TG183B was raced throughout the next season by Warwick and Bruno Giacomelli.

Their performance complemented by the excellent Pirelli radial tyres, Warwick and Toleman gradually had become consistent top six challengers towards the end of the 1983 season, scoring their first Championship points with a fourth place in the Dutch Grand Prix at Zandvoort.

In 1984, Warwick decided to accelerate his own F1 career prospects by joining the Renault works team, then a leading grand prix force. His place in the Toleman-Hart line-up was taken by a dynamic young Brazilian by the name of Ayrton Senna. That season – his first in F1, at the wheel of the brilliant Toleman-Hart TG184 – Senna firmly gave notice of his future greatness with a stupendous second place at Monaco where he was closing relentlessly on Alain Prost's leading McLaren-TAG when the race was prematurely flagged to a halt at half distance on a near flooded track.

Senna would follow that up with third place in both the British Grand Prix at Brands Hatch and the Portuguese race at Estoril, confirming

Warwick in animated discussion with Rory Byrne and Pat Symonds in the Imola pits. (Formula One Pictures)

Alex Hawkridge, Toleman's Managing Director, with Derek Warwick. Hawkridge was the driving force behind the Toleman F1 operation. (Formula One Pictures)

his status as one of the most exciting new F1 talents of the decade.

Unfortunately, by this time it was clear that Toleman was in trouble. At the start of the 1984 season they had switched from Pirelli to Michelin rubber in a move which caused a degree of bad feeling with the Italian tyre company. Then, at the end of 1984, Michelin pulled out of F1. Goodyear could not service Toleman and Pirelli would not. The dilemma was only resolved by Toleman purchasing the Pirelli tyre contract owned by the tiny Spirit team, which then withdrew from F1. All this happened in time for the 1985 Monaco Grand Prix after Benetton, by now tiring of its parallel involvement with the increasingly hopeless Alfa Romeos, took over as sponsors with Teo Fabi behind the

wheel. It was, as things transpired, a halfway house to taking over the company the following year.

During the 1985 season the new 'United Colors of Benetton' identification was also displayed on the Hart turbo-engined Toleman TG185s. Brian Hart was short on development budget, but there were a few bright moments, most notably Fabi qualified on pole position for the German Grand Prix at the new Nurburgring. Admittedly, the shy Italian had timed his fastest run to perfection between rain showers, and in the race had to retire with clutch problems,but it was a excellent showing nevertheless.

Those early season problems tended to mask the innovative specification of the TG185 chassis which featured an aerodynamic 'step' beneath the monocoque which Byrne had developed thanks to exclusive use of the Royal Military College wind tunnel at Shrivenham. This novel configuration enhanced the aerodynamic download developed without the penalty of additional drag. In many ways, this was a crucial F1 design turning point for the 1980s, the significance of which was perhaps disguised by the car's overall unreliability.

Toleman failed to score a single point in the 1985 Constructors' Championship and, during the course of the season, decided to sell out to Benetton. Thus the Witney-based team moved smoothly into the next stage of its commercial development under the Benetton family name.

For an organisation whose knitwear products have primarily been aimed at a young and vigorous sector of the buying public, a glamorous sporting activity such as F1 could only enhance Benetton's vibrant image. The company had previously been involved in sponsorship of handball, basketball and rugby teams, but the global status of motorsport in particular, with its vast television audiences, offered itself as the most attractive promotional medium at a time when Benetton was undergoing dramatic worldwide commercial expansion.

In July 1985 the team also acquired a new team manager in the person of Peter Collins, by then a seasoned F1 hand who had previously worked for

Making progress. Engine wizard Brian Hart talks to Toleman's young ace Ayrton Senna early in 1984. (Formula One Pictures)

the established top line Lotus and Williams operations. An Australian born in Sydney, he had been brought up living only a short distance from the Warwick Farm circuit which would host many rounds of the prestigious Tasman Championship during his teenage years in the mid-1960s.

'My interest had been sparked off by my brother, who was acting as a mechanic to a friend's racing team,' he recalled, 'and it didn't take me long to realise that I wanted to become part of the scene. Not as a mechanic, because I didn't have the right sort of qualifications, but something perhaps on the administrative side.'

After trying his hand in the travel business and journalism, Collins also acted as a part-time press liaison officer for Warwick Farm which was being run by the expatriate Englishman Geoff Sykes. He was quick to admit that Sykes helped him enormously when it came to developing a lot of contacts within the British motor racing industry.

Transitional phase. Backing from United Colors of Benetton got Toleman's TG185 design off to a belated 1985 F1 campaign. This is Teo Fabi at the Nurburgring where he qualified on pole position for that year's German GP. (Formula One Pictures)

Collins made a breakthrough in 1978 when he began a long series of interviews with Lotus, eventually joining the famous Norfolk-based squad as assistant team manager the following year. Ultimately he rose to the status of team manager, although he reflected that 'they didn't seem to like official titles there'.

At the start of 1982 he spent a short spell managing the ATS team before being invited by Frank Williams to join his team as racing manager. He held this position for three years until the approach from Benetton arrived.

'Rory Byrne was asked to talk to me at Monaco that year,' he recalled. 'At that stage Benetton only had a minor shareholding in the team, but it was pretty clear which way things were going. This was very important to me because I needed to be sure that the team's future was secure and properly financed before making such an important career decision. But I was convinced.'

From the start of 1986, the team was officially renamed Benetton Formula. Hart had been replaced by BMW as the engine supplier. The drivers Gerhard Berger and Teo Fabi looked suitably competitive and the team picked up several World Championship points in the early races before

'What does this guy from the outside know?'

On 21 August 1989, Peter Collins resigned as Benetton's team manager. His place was assumed by his former assistant Gordon Message who had been responsible for the hands-on, day-to-day management of the F1 operation ever since 1984. Message had developed excellent organisational abilities within the company, but this change in management structure was supplemented by the arrival of a new Benetton nominee appointed to head up the team's commercial activities. His name was Flavio Briatore.

Here was something of a culture shock for the F1 traditionalists. Briatore, an accomplished sportsman, had worked for two years as a ski instructor in the Italian Alps, before moving to a leading insurance company, then the Stock Exchange of Milan, and thence to a business career that included a spell as the personal assistant to company co-founder Luciano Benetton. In 1977 he moved to the US to run a real estate business, subsequently spending seven years setting up Benetton's retail operation there. 'It was very difficult,' he remembered. 'Nobody knew much about us. I began to think that the only Italian the average American had heard of was Rudolph Valentino. But we had a very aggressive strategy and, after only five years, had something like 750 stores in the US.'

In 1988 Briatore planned to take a year's sabbatical. 'I went to my house in the Virgin Islands, but after two weeks I had a phone call from Luciano telling me to meet him in New York. I asked him what this was about. "We're going to Australia for the race," he replied. I said, "what race?" He told me, "the Formula 1 race."'

This was the 1988 Australian GP at Adelaide which acted as a trailer for Briatore's increasing involvement in the Benetton F1 operation. Yet what Flavio found when he took on the job was not totally to his liking.

'Immediately I arrived in F1, I realised something was wrong. It was clear to me that grand prix racing was no longer sport, but business. F1 had become media- and television-dependent, but nobody seemed to be trying to do anything to improve the show. Journalists would come to me and shrug, "that was just another boring race." Sure enough, the next day you would open the paper and read, "yes, the race was boring, forget it." This was no good to anybody.'

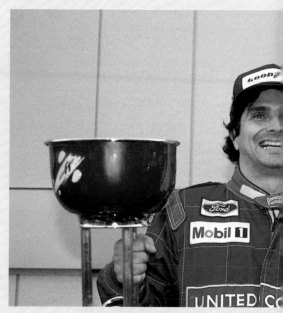

Many F1 establishment figures felt that as a newcomer Briatore didn't respect the rules. He could understand that. 'When you are in a business, any business, you think you are the best. There is a tendency to think "what does this guy from the outside know? He has no experience." The mentality was that if you are not part of the old generation, you have no knowledge. You are nobody. You don't understand.

'My response to that was, "no, perhaps it's you guys who don't understand."'

Briatore made great play of the fact that he knew nothing about the intricacies of F1. A race anorak he most definitely was not. But back-to-back World Championships in 1994 and 1995 spoke for themselves. So did the media hype the team and its chief enjoyed. Sleek, chic and permanently tanned, Briatore relished the high life which went with his role, particularly the lifestyle magazine features which were attracted to the self-generated air of mystery which surrounded him. He also became a close personal friend of FIA Vice President Bernie Ecclestone and, indeed, purchased Bernie's former London flat overlooking the Thames at Cheyne Walk.

After the glory years with Michael Schumacher, then the doldrums that followed, Briatore eventually quit Benetton late in 1997. His position was taken by David Richards, founder of the specialist Prodrive rally preparation concern. Their management styles were dramatically different.

Briatore with his boys. Flavio poses with Nelson Piquet and Roberto Moreno after the two Brazilians posted a Benetton 1–2 in the 1990 Japanese GP at Suzuka. (Formula One Pictures)

running into a lean patch mid-way through the year.

The single turbo, four-cylinder 1.5-litre BMW engines developed prodigious power – in excess of 1000 horsepower when running in high boost qualifying trim – but could also prove frail and mechanically unreliable. However, Gerhard Berger drove brilliantly to win the Mexican Grand Prix in torrid conditions which decisively favoured the Pirelli tyres. The team finished the year with sixth place in the Constructors' title.

The top brass were panicked into standing Herbert down

A key turning point in the Benetton team's history came at the start of 1987 when it was decided to switch to Ford power. The team took over supplies of the 120-degree V6 turbo which had been used by the Haas Lola F1 team the previous season. Although not the most obviously powerful of the turbo generation, its wide cylinder angle enabled it to be packaged extremely tightly within the B187 chassis which made for a notably effective aerodynamic profile.

Additional development progress was made with the Ford turbo throughout the 1987 season during which Fabi had been joined in the driver line-up by Thierry Boutsen, the popular Belgian replacing Gerhard Berger who had gone off to Ferrari.

Boutsen and Fabi both made it to lower placings on the rostrum during the course of the season, finishing eighth and ninth in the Drivers' championship and helping the team to earn 28 points – and fifth place – in the Constructors' contest.

It is a matter of debate just how close the Ford V6 turbo came to winning its first grand prix in a Benetton. Nobody will ever know, because its development was brought to an abrupt halt – in Ford's view – by another change in the F1 engine regulations. The days of the turbo had suddenly become numbered and normally aspirated engines, this time of 3.5-litres capacity, which had been readmitted to F1 in 1987, would be the only permitted power source from 1989 onwards.

Ford immediately made the switch to the new Cosworth-built DFR engine development programme for Benetton in 1988, although the benefit of hindsight now suggests that they would have done better sticking with the turbo, even under the regulations requiring only 150-litres of fuel capacity and boost pressure of 2.5-bar. Had Benetton's B188 used the Ford turbo in 1988 it is quite possible that Honda would not have exacted the level of dominance which carried the McLaren team to victory in 15 out of the 16 races, an all-time record.

At the start of 1989, Benetton had another change in its driver line-up. Just as Fabi had been replaced by the highly rated Alessandro Nannini at the beginning of the previous year, now Thierry Boutsen had accepted an offer to join Williams. His place was taken by Johnny Herbert, the young

Gerhard Berger's Benetton-BMW B186 makes a tyre stop during the 1986 German GP at Hockenheim. (Formula One Pictures)

Englishman who was very much a protégé of Collins.

Herbert's recruitment to Benetton was controversial. The baby-faced Essex lad had won the 1987 British Formula 3 Championship in fine style at the wheel of an Eddie Jordan team Reynard, then moved up into Formula 3000 at the start of the following season. Courted briefly by Team Lotus, he had produced some impressive lap times at a Monza test session in a Lotus-Honda 100T only weeks before smashing both his feet in a terrible racing accident at Brands Hatch in the F3000 Reynard.

Herbert's feet were so badly damaged that it was thought he might never walk again, let alone drive. But he fought hard to recover and was duly included in the Benetton line-up from the beginning of 1989. Despite being unable to apply full pressure to the brake pedal and, like Nannini, handicapped by being obliged to start the year driving the old B188, Johnny came home a superb fourth on his debut F1 outing in the Brazilian GP at Rio.

The team had started the year using the old B188 and it was several races into the season by the time the new Cosworth Ford HB-propelled B189 eventually supplanted the DFR-engined car. By the time the new machine was developed, Herbert's spell with the team had run out.

Peter Collins was Benetton's team manager from 1985 to 1989. (Formula One Pictures)

Benetton switched from BMW power to use the Ford turbo V6 engine at the start of the 1987 season. (Formula One Pictures)

Unfortunately his form spiralled downwards after Brazil and, despite a fifth place at Phoenix, he was officially stood down from the team after failing to qualify in Canada. The Benetton and Ford top brass were panicked into 'resting' the Englishman for three months – F1 euphemism for giving him the bullet in favour of Benetton nominee Emanuele Pirro. As things transpired, the Italian driver proved rather less obviously talented than the Briton he replaced.

In 1989, Benetton's newly appointed F1 chief Flavio Briatore was determined to bring a more extrovert lifestyle focus into the world of grand prix racing. But for the moment, there was an immediate problem to deal with. The season was not developing well for the team.

Team leader Nannini's morale had initially been dented by Herbert's fine showing at Rio although he had also finished in the points. Then came a third at Imola and fourth in Mexico. But at Phoenix, despite qualifying a superb third fastest, he crashed heavily in the race morning warm-up and had to retire from the race after only ten laps suffering from exhaustion. He drove well in the French Grand Prix, holding third and second places during the early stages only to retire with suspension problems. That was followed by a fine third place at Silverstone, fifth at Spa in the pouring rain, then fourth at Estoril.

Then came the 1989 Japanese Grand Prix at Suzuka, a race which has gone down in the F1 history books as the scene of the controversial collision between the McLaren-Hondas of Alain Prost and Ayrton Senna under braking for the chicane before the pits. Senna went on to win on the road, but was disqualified for rejoining the race by driving past the chicane, rather than re-tracing his steps and actually negotiating this tight turn.

As a direct result of this, Nannini inherited his first grand prix victory by 12 seconds from the Williams-Renault of Riccardo Patrese. He followed that up a fortnight later with a splendid run to second place in monsoon-like conditions at Adelaide, following Thierry Boutsen's Williams past the chequered flag at the end of the Australian Grand Prix. Emanuele Pirro took fifth in the second Benetton B189 to round off a season which had started on a shaky note, improving only towards the end.

Nannini was left with sixth place in the Drivers' World Championship on 32 points while Benetton took fourth in the Constructors' table on 39 points. It was well ahead of the fifth place Tyrrell's tally of 16, but, by the same token, light years away from McLaren's title winning 141. There was still a great deal of work to do.

For the 1990 season Nelson Piquet was chosen as Benetton's number one driver with the team now also benefiting from former Ferrari designer John Barnard's appointment as Technical Director. Barnard broadly inherited the basic design of the new B190 challenger but had sufficient input into its final configuration to be quite happy with the end result.

Barnard replaced Rory Byrne at the Benetton design helm after the South African, together with race engineer

Thierry Boutsen's Benetton-Ford B187 in the 1987 Belgian GP at Spa Francorchamps where he retired from his home race. (Formula One Pictures)

Pat Symonds, had moved off to work on what proved to be the stillborn Reynard F1 project. Barnard concentrated a lot of his efforts on attempting to make the new B190 less pitch sensitive than Byrne's cars had traditionally tended to be and, sure enough, the new car proved to be less nervous than its immediate predecessors.

For the second successive year the team had the exclusive use of the Cosworth-Ford HB V8 which was gradually developed during the course of the season to produce around 625bhp at around 12,500rpm.

Piquet displayed consistency and dependability for much of the season, while Alessandro Nannini was developing into a well-rounded performer at the wheel of the second B190. Then came disaster. Just as his career was looking so promising, the genial Italian driver was involved in a helicopter accident prior to the Japanese Grand Prix. The craft crashed during an attempt to land near his parents' home and Nannini's right arm was severed below the elbow. After ten hours of micro-surgery in a Florence hospital, the limb was successfully re-attached, but Sandro's F1 racing days were over.

For the Japanese race, Benetton was successful in securing the services of Piquet's compatriot Roberto Moreno as second driver, the EuroBrun team obligingly releasing him from his existing contract. Moreno arrived just in time to round off a 1–2 Benetton victory at Suzuka, following Nelson across the line after Senna's McLaren

Launch of the distinctively liveried Benetton-Ford B188 at a stylish London studio was typical of the extrovert media events held under Flavio Briatore's direction. (Formula One Pictures)

Alessandro Nannini was Benetton's second driver in 1988, the smoking, coffee-drinking Italian extrovert becoming a great favourite with the team personnel. (Formula One Pictures)

Flavio Briatore, Alessandro Nannini (middle) and Nelson Piquet at an Estoril test session, 1989. (Formula One Pictures)

had rammed Prost's Ferrari off the circuit at the start of the race, and Nigel Mansell's Ferrari had broken a driveshaft in the pit lane as it accelerated away after a tyre stop.

By the start of the 1991 season, John Barnard was well into his perfectionist stride, but the debut of the new car slipped behind its original schedule with the result that Piquet and Moreno were obliged to use uprated versions of the B190 for the first two races at Phoenix and Interlagos.

The B191 was built round a totally new monocoque, the product of a complex carbon-fibre composite manufacturing process which enabled Barnard to do away with the need for

Hiring Nelson Piquet, seen here at Hockenheim, for 1990 was a shrewd move by Benetton. The veteran triple World Champion would win two races with the Ford-engined B191, the last ones of the season. (Formula One Pictures)

load-carrying internal bracketry and bulkheads. It also marked a fundamental departure from his previous philosophy of not having the aerodynamic flexibility of totally removable upper bodywork.

Although designed from the outset to run with a semi-automatic gearchange and computer-controlled active suspension, the car eventually raced through the year with a manual six-speed transmission and conventional suspension. The team also switched from Goodyear to Pirelli rubber at the start of 1991, but this would yield just a single lucky victory when Piquet overtook Nigel Mansell's ailing Williams on the last lap of the Canadian Grand Prix at Montreal.

Yet in the wake of that race, Benetton looked set to be riven by a controversial split when it was announced that John Barnard would be leaving the team. The British engineer felt frustrated when it became clear

33

that the team was reluctant to proceed with the building of a new factory which had originally been agreed. Briatore, for his part, reportedly found Barnard excessively demanding to work for and felt he was attempting to exert undue influence in areas which were not his specific responsibility.

An even more glittering prize lay a few weeks down the road

Yet scarcely had Barnard cleared his desk than it was announced at the British Grand Prix that Benetton would be on the receiving end of a major shake-up with Tom Walkinshaw taking over control of all aspects of the team's engineering efforts.

Walkinshaw, whose TWR organisation had made quite a reputation building Jaguar's Le Mans-winning sports cars, also took a 35 per cent stake in the Benetton company with the prospect of another 15 per cent to follow in due course.

The rugged Scot had previously admitted that he wanted TWR to become involved in F1 eventually and the Benetton link-up looked the best way available. 'There is no attraction for me to go into F1 just to make up the numbers. I couldn't cope with that. The top teams in F1 are not only extremely professional, but they can also draw on an enormous data base from which to sort out the problems they encounter on the various tracks.

'Now we have got the opportunity of becoming involved in a well-funded team with a core of good people. We've talked it all through with the Benetton family and they clearly want to remain involved. They want us involved because they wanted to strengthen the race team, but they knew we would not become involved uneless we were part-owners of the company.'

The Walkinshaw/Benetton partnership looked like developing into a fascinating alliance. Yet there was an even more glittering prize for the team lurking a few weeks down the road in the form of a mild-mannered 22-year old German who had yet to step into the cockpit of an F1 car for the first time.

Chapter 2

Schumacher's championship glory

Michael Schumacher has always been a confident competitor. 'I remember well when somebody gave me the opportunity to test a Formula Ford car,' he laughs, 'and he said "the guy is very quick in karting, but he will never be quick in a Formula car, because the driving style is so different. " I think he was a little bit wrong there.'

The German had a boyish outward manner which concealed the sort of steely resolve and ruthless commitment associated with Ayrton Senna. However, if Schumacher lacked Senna's ascetic, almost messianic style, projecting instead a freshly scrubbed and more obvious outward enthusiasm, he has successfully laid claim to the Brazilian driver's crown at the very pinnacle of his chosen sport. Quite an achievement for a lad from a modest background who, scarcely more than ten years ago, was scrambling round a little go-kart circuit in the German town of Kerpen where his mother ran the hamburger stand.

Born on 3 January 1969, Michael won the 1984 German Junior Kart Championship to set himself on the road to fame and fortune. Three years later he had won the senior German and European crowns, followed the next season by victory in the German domestic Formula Koenig car racing series, second place in the European Formula Ford Championship, and fourth place in the German FF series.

In 1989 he graduated to the German F3 series driving a Reynard for the team run by his long-time manager Willi Weber, a shrewd businessman who recognised that this youngster had dynamic potential. How right he was. Mercedes-Benz quickly became interested in Schumacher and in 1990 he was recruited to drive for the highly professional Sauber-Mercedes junior driver team – alongside Heinz-Harald Frentzen and Karl Wendlinger – in the Sports Car World Championships. He also won the German F3 Championship that year. This was the crucial launch pad from which Michael Schumacher's career took off with such spectacular effect.

People liked seeing a winner enjoying himself on the podium

At the 1991 Belgian Grand Prix, Michael was invited to drive for the Jordan F1 team, then in its maiden grand prix season and making quite a mark. He lined up alongside the Italian Andrea de Cesaris, the German standing in for regular team driver Bertrand Gachot who had recently been jailed in Britain following a traffic incident where he had used a CS gas canister in a dispute with a London taxi driver.

Despite his previous achievements, Schumacher had never driven an F1 car before. Inevitably, this meant that he was something of an unknown quantity, but when he qualified seventh fastest at Spa, not only ahead of de Cesaris but also in front of Benetton driver Roberto Moreno, it was clear that he had made an outstanding impression.

Michael's first F1 race ended after only a single corner as the Jordan's clutch packed up, but already the young German was hot property. One man for whom the Belgian race had merely been further confirmation of what he'd already expected was Benetton engineering boss Tom Walkinshaw. He had seen Schumacher

racing the Mercedes sports cars against his own Jaguars and suspected then that he was something really special. Now Walkinshaw was certain.

The fortnight separating the Belgian and Italian Grands Prix saw frantic negotiations to get Schumacher out of his Jordan contract and into a Benetton. With Bernie Ecclestone taking a hand in the contractual comings and goings, the deal was eventually done, leaving Eddie Jordan temporarily humiliated and vowing legal retribution.

Roberto Moreno was duly replaced in the Benetton squad, briefly taking over Schumacher's vacated Jordan, and Michael found himself lining up alongside Nelson Piquet who was about to celebrate his 200th grand prix. By now one was tempted to suggest that the veteran Brazilian was past his best but, while he could perhaps no longer demonstrate the sort of form which had carried him to three

World Championships in the 1980s, his huge experience would prove helpful to young Schumacher.

At Monza, Michael started as he meant to go on, out-running Piquet all weekend to finish fifth in the race, just over 11 sec ahead. The rest of the 1991 season went quite smoothly for Schumacher, who finished sixth in both Portugal and Spain, but retired with engine problems in Japan, and followed that with a collision with Alesi in Australia. Perhaps not the way he would have liked to end his first F1 season, but he had shown sufficient star quality for Flavio Briatore to

Great new talent. Michael Schumacher was signed up to replace Moreno for the 1991 Italian GP at Monza. (Formula One Pictures)

Schumacher at the 1991 Australian GP; he retired after crashing with Jean Alesi, but even with only six F1 races under his belt, had marked himself out as somebody very special. (Formula One Pictures)

decide to build the team round him for the following season.

In 1992 Schumacher finished eight of the first 11 races in the top four. Then, in Belgium, exactly one year after his spectacular debut at the wheel of a Jordan, he took his maiden victory in treacherously wet/dry conditions winning by nearly 40 sec from poleman Nigel Mansell's Williams Renault.

It was an excellent performance from the young ace and many found it refreshing to see a driver actually enjoying himself on the podium after winning a race, for he was jumping around all over the place with a huge smile on his face. This delight was a quality that would endure.

The autumn of 1992 had also seen Benetton go up a gear with a switch from its rather confined headquarters at Witney, in Oxfordshire, to a new, 17-acre, 85,000 square foot factory at nearby Enstone. This brought a hitherto rather fragmented operation under a single roof. Engineering Director Tom Walkinshaw and Technical Director Ross Brawn quickly had the new regime drilled into a well-ordered state and it began to seem as though Benetton was now close to having marshalled the technical resources necessary to compete with F1's established front runners.

Meanwhile, Schumacher ended his first full season of Formula 1 third in the drivers' title with 53 points. He had

Martin Brundle never quite realised his potential as Schumacher's Benetton team-mate in 1992. He might have won the 1992 Canadian GP at Montreal had it not been for a transmission failure on his Benetton B192. (Formula One Pictures)

nearly got a second victory in Adelaide, when he ran closely behind the winner Gerhard Berger for the whole of the last 30 laps. However, that satisfaction would have to wait until the Portuguese Grand Prix in September 1993, where he beat the two Williams drivers Alain Prost and Damon Hill to the flag. Schumacher finished fourth in the 1993 championship, but his best seasons were yet to come – 1994 would prove to be the turning point in his career.

At the start of 1994 there seemed nothing extraordinary to mark out Benetton's potential as a World Championship winning force. But changes had gone on behind the scene that were immediately obvious from the touchlines. Cosworth's partnership with Ford saw an all-new engine, the Zetec-R V8, which replaced the HB, now at the end of its potential.

There were other changes on the cards for this season, most notably the FIA's decision to ban a wide range of driver aids such as active suspension, traction control and anti-lock braking systems. Refuelling also returned, which emphasised the importance of strategy in winning races. Yet for Benetton, the year started with worries as to whether or not Cosworth could wring sufficient power from the new Ford V8.

'We had worked on the HB for four years and squeezed everything out of it that we could,' said Martin Walters, Cosworth's Chief Development

Brundle's great day came two races later when he finished third in the British GP at Silverstone; here he joins Williams drivers Nigel Mansell and Riccardo Patrese on the podium. (Formula One Pictures)

Right Tom Walkinshaw joined Benetton as Engineering Director, his TWR operation taking a stake in the team. (Formula One Pictures)

Michael Schumacher with his shrewd and far-sighted business manager Willi Weber (centre), the man who has helped make the young German a multi-millionaire. (Formula One Pictures)

Engineer. 'It had performance limitations which became more obvious the more work we did on it. Mechanically it was very difficult to run beyond 13,500rpm. We had big-end bearing problems which were not a simple thing to solve. It really needed a major re-design.

'What we did was to ask what sort of power we could get out of a V8 if we ran it to 14,500rpm, and what sort of performance that would give us. It looked mechanically possible. We had to go for much larger bores, larger than we had been to before, and that made us worry about combustion.

'But we got the work done early in time to allow the team to test early, although we had to limit the engines to 125 miles before changing them. It was the first time I turned up at the season opener with Benetton having been in a position to complete its full winter testing schedule.'

Many people felt that Ford was being unduly conservative sticking with the V8 cylinder configuration at a time when most of its opposition was opting for the V10 route. But Cosworth's then Racing Manager Dick Scammell was confident they had chosen the right route.

'Continuing the V8 configuration was a decision taken jointly by the whole engineering group at Cosworth, together with the Benetton management,' he explained. 'Even Bernard Dudot of Renault [the French engine maker's highly respected F1 technical chief] said to me that if we can get our engine to run at the same speed as their V10, then we're going to win races.

I always felt that Senna would win the title, not me

The new 65-degree Zetec-R V8 owed nothing in terms of shared parts to its predecessor and the new engine benefited greatly from many of the technical lessons learned from the planned Ford V12 F1 programme, which by then had been suspended, most notably in the areas of heat rejection, crankshaft configuration and the use of ceramics in the cylinder head design.

Employing titanium con-rods and magnesium alloy pistons, the Ford Zetec-R was designed to run at speeds which, if achieved, should have matched the performance targets set by Renault.

This optimism was shared by the Benetton design staff headed by Ross Brawn, Rory Byrne and Pat Symonds, now returned to the team, who developed the new B194 chassis as a logical development of the previous year's machine.

Prior to the first race of 1994, the team's new number two driver J. J. Lehto suffered a major testing accident at Silverstone which left him sidelined with cracked vetebrae in his neck. It was a disaster from which the popular Finn never quite recovered, for although he returned to F1 mid-season, he could never quite match Schumacher's pace.

Schumacher started the season apparently set to go head-to-head with Ayrton Senna for the World Championship. The brilliant Brazilian triple World Champion had switched to the Williams team after six years with McLaren and was determined to continue in the title-winning vein established by Nigel Mansell and Alain Prost in 1992/93.

The season opened at Senna's home circuit, Interlagos at Sao Paulo. For the local hero it didn't go well. Nor ever would again. Schumacher won the Brazilian Grand Prix in decisive style, Senna spinning off in the closing stages of the race as he battled to keep pace with his young rival. That was followed by a second win in the Pacific Grand Prix at Japan's TI Aida circuit – Senna spun off on the first corner – and a third win in the tragic San Marino Grand Prix at Imola where Senna crashed fatally while running ahead of the Benetton team leader.

Later in the season, having clinched his first World Championship in acutely controversial circumstances, Schumacher would dedicate his title to Senna.

This autograph-signing is a hot business, especially when you have congratulations to contend with too. (Formula One Pictures)

44

You calculate and you analyse. (Formula One Pictures)

Right *Celebrating a controversial success. The Benetton crew after Michael Schumacher clinched the 1994 World Championship at Adelaide.* (Formula One Pictures)

Horror show. The pit lane conflagration which enveloped Jos Verstappen's Benetton B194 when refuelling went wrong during the 1994 German Grand Prix. (Formula One Pictures)

'What happened at Imola was just a nightmare,' he said. 'All of us knew what sort of feelings we had about this, but it was always clear to me in my own mind that I was not going to win the Championship, but that Ayrton was going to win. So I would like to take this Championship and give it to him. It is the right thing now to give something which I achieved – which he should have achieved – to him.'

No good reason was given for the attempt to hide this system

Pretty words. In the meantime, there was to be all sorts of doubt and innuendo cast over the Benetton team's efforts throughout the 1994 season. The Championship campaign had started with many team managers predicting that the FIA, motor racing's governing body, did not have the technical resources necessary to police its ban on driver aids. As things transpired, this was largely fair as, by Hockenheim, the pit lane was only just discovering about potential problems with the electronic boxes taken from the first three finishers at Imola.

A detailed examination of the Benetton's electronic control systems revealed that it had a 'launch control' facility, although the team insisted that, even if this had not been deleted from the software, it had been disarmed. The FIA chose to release part of Technical Delegate Charlie Whiting's Imola report which confirmed that the Benetton B194 did indeed have such a control system, although he added the rider, 'the best evidence is that the team did not use it.'

The launch control system would enable the driver to initiate the start with a single action as it controlled clutch, gearshift and engine speed fully automatically to a predetermined pattern. In order to activate the system it was necessary to select a particular menu with ten options on a lap-top PC screen plugged into the car's electronic management system.

The ten options showed on the PC screen. If one then scrolled down beyond the tenth listed item, to the unlisted option 13, the launch control system could be activated. As the FIA noted darkly 'no satisfactory explanation was offered for this apparent attempt to conceal the feature.'

It was also pointed out by the FIA that the driver had to work through a particular sequence of gearshift paddle positions, as well as clutch and throttle positions, in order to activate the launch control system. The strong implication here was that the driver would have to be a willing accomplice in the event of such a system being employed. But Benetton stuck to its insistence that the system was only used in testing.

Rival teams regarded the FIA's judgement with some scepticism. In particular, they had seen Schumacher's spectacular start from the second row of the French Grand Prix at Magny-Cours, where he dodged between the two Williams FW16s of Damon Hill

Whole in one

Motorsport drivers hone their skill to such a pitch in their own field that you wonder if, lobster like, they might be correspondingly weak in other areas. Not according to David Richards. 'The qualities that make a great sportsman are the same across many disciplines. You would probably find that if you took a Michael Schumacher at a young age and put him into another sporting discipline which required similar physical and mental attributes he would do just as well.

'You tend to find that good sportsmen are good sportsmen, it's as simple as that.

You can take a grand prix driver onto a golf course or a clay pigeon shoot and they will be good.

'There is this common denominator across many sports but, above anything else, it is the unique self-belief which is so essential in any form of motorsport where you are actually putting everything on the limit. You really have to believe in yourself to do that.'

The commonality is obvious in rallying and F1. 'Colin McRae tested a Jordan, for example, a couple of years ago and took to it like a fish to water. At the same time Martin Brundle tried one of our Subaru rally cars and did just the same.'

Gifted in many disciplines Michael Schumacher takes the chequered flag to win the 1994 French GP with the Ford V8-engined Benetton B194. (Formula One Pictures)

Michael wins the 1995 Spanish GP and faces the usual media scrutiny. (Formula One Pictures)

Great partnerships. Schumacher with his race engineer Pat Symonds at the 1995 British GP at Silverstone, and with fiancée Corinna Betsch. (Formula One Pictures)

and Nigel Mansell to take an immediate and unchallenged lead. There were, felt the critics, more than a few passing doubts on this score.

Benetton dismissed such queries. 'The risk involved with being caught and eliminated from the Championship is tremendous,' said Ross Brawn. 'If we were foolish enough to use such a system willingly and be caught, we would be putting 200 people and their families' futures at risk.'

Briatore paid the price for questioning FIA competence

Yet Benetton's management style at this time was certainly arrogant, even bordering on confrontational. At the height of the safety controversy in the wake of Ayrton Senna's fatal accident, Flavio Briatore wrote to FIA President Max Mosley questioning the governing body's competence to administer F1 properly. This was an extremely risky strategy for which Briatore paid the price – his own acute embarrassment within the F1 community – when the correspondence was leaked to certain newspapers, perhaps by the FIA.

There was more aggravation to follow at the British Grand Prix. On the final parade lap, Schumacher breached the rules by overtaking Damon Hill's Williams. Out went the board indicating that Michael was due a stop-go penalty, but the German driver stayed out in the lead while Walkinshaw and Briatore argued the toss with the race stewards.

In the end, Schumacher found himself disqualified from the race and lost the six Championship points for his second place. Schumacher was also given a two race ban, but the team lodged an appeal which at least allowed him to race before his home crowd at Hockenheim in the German Grand Prix a fortnight later. However, on appeal Benetton's fine was upped from $25,000 to $500,000 for their failure to obey the instructions of race officials.

As it happened, there was even more discomfort awaiting the Benetton team at Hockenheim. Schumacher's car retired with engine failure – and the nightmare which everyone in the F1 pit lane had been dreading ever since in-race refuelling had been re-introduced, suddenly became reality as Jos Verstappen stopped his fifth place Benetton at the end of lap 15.

It should have been a routine refuelling stop, but a malfunction of the rig resulted in fuel continuing to flow once the hose had been uncoupled from the car. Television viewers across the world just had time to register the fact that fuel was suddenly splashing over the side of the Benetton before the car erupted into a horrifying fireball. The conflagration was snuffed out with commendable speed, but Verstappen and five mechanics suffered burns although, thanks to their fire protection suits, these were thankfully superficial.

Great moment. Johnny Herbert celebrates victory at Silverstone, his first win, and before an ecstatic home crowd. (Formula One Pictures)

His ambition is no idol threat

One of the Benetton team's PR publications suggested that if Hollywood was really considering a grand prix blockbuster then 1998 driver Giancarlo Fisichella would be ideal to play the role of a top racing driver. Even if he wasn't one already!

But although Giancarlo may look like a Latin matinee idol, there had never been any doubt in his own mind that he wanted an active part in the thick of the F1 action. And not just as the love interest either.

'My father was a big F1 fan and I used to watch the races on television with him,' he remembers. 'He passed his passion on to me and when I was little, Niki Lauda was my hero. Then, when I was eight, I went to watch a kart race near my home in Rome and saw that kids my age were racing.

'I wanted to have a go and asked my Papa to buy me a kart. He did, and that was it. From that day on I wanted to be a grand prix driver.'

Fisichella freely admits that he had some fortunate breaks on his way to the top. After starring in both the Italian and international karting scene, he won the 1994 Monaco F3 classic and the 1994 Italian F3 Championship, then spent two seasons driving for Alfa Romeo in the German Touring Car Championship and the International Touring Car Series. He also worked as a test driver for the Italian F1 team Minardi in 1995 and for Ferrari the following year. In 1996, as reserve driver for Minardi, he contested eight grands prix. As a Jordan driver in 1997 he immedi-ately caused a quickening of interest by leading the German GP and finishing on the podium in Canada and Belgium.

'I think I am a lucky lad,' he says with some candour. 'I have always made a point of driving as hard as I could and pushing to the maximum, and if I am honest, I always thought that I would succeed, so the dream quickly became a reality.'

He believes that his spectacular success in karting was the key to his whole career. 'Karting is not the only way to get to the top, because there are examples like Villeneuve and Hill who did not bother, but I feel it is the best school a driver can attend. However, others have proved that if their destiny lies with motor racing, then they will make it even without karting. Now when I get the chance I still race karts for fun.'

The fact that Giancarlo has already driven for three F1 teams by the age of 25 reflects just how highly he has come to be regarded. 'There are huge differences between Minardi, Jordan and Benetton,' he reflects. 'Minardi is very small and somehow they keep going in F1. I owe Giancarlo Minardi a huge debt because it is thanks to him that I am in F1.

'There is less of a difference between the Jordan and Benetton teams. Benetton has a great atmosphere to it and the team is incredibly professional. It has a strong will to win and, most importantly, it has the means to do that.

'Even though most of the staff are English, the heart of this team is Italian, the Benetton family is Italian and the team's entrance licence is Italian.'

Fisichella's 1998 form has come as no surprise to Jordan's Commercial Director

Ian Phillips. 'The thing that impressed me enormously about Giancarlo was how strong his mentality was. He was paired with Ralf Schumacher for 1997 and during pre-season testing Ralf looked extremely strong. Then, after the first race, Giancarlo went testing at Silverstone where he crashed very heavily at Stowe corner in the wet and fractured his knee cap.

'He was barely fit enough to drive in the second race in Brazil and there were some people who believed this would be the end of him. But he out-qualified Ralf at Interlagos, only to get taken out by him in Argentina. This was a set-back from which he recovered with a display of mental strength the like of which I have never seen before from an Italian driver.'

Fisichella spends much of his time in Oxford in order to be in close contact with the Benetton factory at Enstone. 'Rome is my home, where I have all my family, my friends and my girlfriend. I know how the city works, so I miss it when I am not there.

'However, in Oxford I like the nice house I have as it is very quiet and calm. I would not like to live in London because there is too much traffic – just like Rome I suppose, but I know where I am going in Rome. If I could change anything about my English home it would be the weather.'

When he is not deeply immersed in the business of testing or racing, Fisichella likes to relax away from the F1 frenzy playing football or tennis and he also enjoys skiing and fishing. 'In Rome I play soccer with my friends. It's not a serious match, but always great fun.'

Film star looks but a real racer at heart. (ICN UK Bureau)

Important preparations. (Formula One Pictures)

Now Benetton found itself embroiled in another drama. A detailed investigation into the cause of the pit fire revealed that a mandatory fuel filter was absent from the Benetton rig, speeding up the fuel flow rate by around one second at the average pit stop. The team claimed it had been removed for the first time in Germany, with due permission from the FIA. The governing body said that this was not the case.

I didn't get the feeling that Hill was bitter about losing the title

In the event, there were sufficient ambiguities to prevent Benetton from being hit with another penalty. Meanwhile Schumacher had been penalised enough. He duly served out his two race suspension by missing the Italian and Portuguese Grands Prix, both of which were won by Damon Hill.

Michael returned to the fray at Jerez where he won the European Grand Prix in storming style. He was then beaten into second place by Hill in the rain-soaked Japanese Grand Prix at Suzuka, then rounded off the season by clinching the 1994 World Championship on an intensely dubious note by apparently ramming Hill out of the Australian Grand Prix at Adelaide.

What made this collision such a particularly contentious issue was the fact that Schumacher had made a crucial driving error when he brushed a wall seconds before colliding with Hill. Did he deliberately take out the Williams driver, knowing that – with just one point to play for – his own title chances were fatally holed? Or was it an inadvertent error, genuinely made?

The following morning the two men met at breakfast time in their hotel restaurant. 'Damon came over and congratulated me and we talked it over,' said Schumacher. 'I did not get the feeling he was bitter about it.' Hill, ever the gentleman, might also have been a better poker player than the German realised.

For the 1995 season Benetton decided to switch to Renault power as the French engine supplier's second works-supported team alongside Williams. On paper this may have seemed an extremely logical move, but there were considerable logistical and technical considerations to be taken into account as Ross Brawn would later reflect.

'We underestimated the problems involved, partly because we had not changed engine supplier for so long,' he said. 'Our 1994 car had been a good one because we had been together as a group at Benetton for three years, plus a much longer period with Cosworth. We had a nice package all round. Renault would prove to be fantastic and it was no disrespect to them when I say that any such transition was bound to be difficult.

'Things didn't quite work out as we'd hoped at first. At the beginning of the season we had a problem with the hydraulic pump drives and there was also a problem with gearbox casings cracking due to vibrational stress. That really set us back quite a bit and we spent the first few races finding our feet. Williams had the advantage to start with.'

In fact, Schumacher opened the season with a victory in the Brazilian Grand Prix at Interlagos, his Benetton B195 heading home David Coulthard's similarly powered Williams FW17. However, even before the race it had been found that a fuel sample from both these cars did not match that which had previously been lodged with the FIA. The two cars thus effectively went to the startline knowing they were in trouble, but after an initial disqualification, the drivers were permitted to keep their Championship points although the Constructors were not.

Hill went on to win both the Argentine and San Marino Grands Prix where, respectively, Schumacher had a third place and an accident on lap 10 while leading. At Imola

Celebrating their second World Championship, a special hug for the boss. (Formula One Pictures)

Schumacher was also subtly admonished by FIA President Max Mosley for trying to circumvent the new rules which required that the all-up weight of a driver and car should be 595kg from the start of the season.

As the cars were now being weighed after the race with the driver not strapped into the cockpit, a heavier 'officially registered' driver weight would have offered potential for running the car lighter during the race. Schumacher tipped the scales at 77kg during the official weigh-in – only to tip the scales at 71.5kg after the Brazilian Grand Prix!

Giving Johnny confidence was not always our highest priority

'I think it is very unfortunate if a World Champion gets involved in a misunderstanding over how much he may or may not weigh at any time in a weekend,' said Mosley sternly. 'It reflects very poorly on the sport and shows a lack of an adult attitude towards it.'

After this shaky start, Schumacher quickly got to grips with his B195, winning in Spain, Monaco and France before being punted off the road at Silverstone as Damon Hill tried an over-ambitious overtaking move in the British Grand Prix.

'What can I say?' shrugged Schumacher. 'I think what Damon did was totally unnecessary. In fact, it was totally stupid. There was no room for two cars and there is no place to overtake there.

'It is such a small straight and even if you brake in the first part, and you turn in, it's almost impossible, and I think if I hadn't been there he would have gone straight on and into the gravel. So he had absolutely no reason to attempt such an overtaking manoeuvre at that time.'

Schumacher's misfortune handed the initiative to his number two driver Johnny Herbert who came through to post his first grand prix victory. He would do precisely the same at Monza after Damon and Michael again tangled during the Italian Grand Prix, but by the same token there was no doubting that the genial English driver had his work cut out competing in the Schumacher-orientated Benetton environment.

'Quite honestly, it was an unfortunate time for Johnny to have joined the team,' admitted Ross Brawn. 'I believe that if he had been with us in 1994, he would have had a much happier season. The fact was that the car was not as good as we would have liked and, when faced with those circumstances, it's difficult to be fair about the responses you have to make to try and sort out the car.

'Given the situation we were in, I think it was proper that we used Michael to try and solve the problems as quickly as possible. He had been driving for us for four years, he was the

Flavio Briatore was a mystery man to many, but his influence certainly brought some added colour to the Benetton team's activities. (Formula One Pictures)

quicker driver and certainly the one with the most experience.

'In fairness to Johnny, the comments he made about the car were correct. It's not that we didn't believe him; we were simply unable to address the things which troubled Johnny as quickly as we should have done, because those problems in some ways did not trouble Michael.

'Confidence level in the car was never a problem for Michael, which meant there were other things that we could get on with sorting out. Giving Johnny confidence in the car was not always our highest priority.

For Benetton, life would never be quite the same again

'I won't pretend that we did a fantastic job for Johnny, but we did the right job for the team under the circumstances we were faced with. As a result, we had a good crack at both Championships and Johnny won two races. There is a lot in Johnny but we were not in a position to get the most out of him. He deserved a lot more credit than perhaps he got for what he did achieve with Benetton in 1995.'

Meanwhile, Schumacher won nine races in total and helped Benetton clinch its first Constructors' Championship crown. The previous year Benetton and Williams had shared the honours, the drivers' crown going to Michael and the constructors' laurels to Williams. This time, however, Benetton marshalled all the efforts at its disposal to clinch both Championships in decisive fashion.

However, for Benetton it was also the end of an era. The Schumacher era. For 1996 Michael would be moving on to a fresh challenge at Ferrari as part of a reputed $25 million deal. Life at Benetton would never be quite the same again.

During Michael's reign there he had grown from being a slightly hesitant young kid to the point where he radiated a taken-for-granted feeling that he is The Best. In so many ways, Michael is the personification of teutonic cool and control. His sense of humour is kept under tight rein. He actually does have a more relaxed side to his character. Away from the pressure-cooker intensity of racing, he will today talk animatedly about his little daughter Gina Maria, born in 1996, his rescue dogs, and how much he and his wife Corinna enjoy the privacy of living in Switzerland.

But when the vizor snaps down on the front of his racing helmet, Michael Schumacher takes on a very different persona. For him, grand prix racing is a matter for analytical concentration – for winning whatever the odds.

Chapter 3

Life after Michael

At the end of the 1995 season Michael Schumacher left Benetton for Ferrari and Johnny Herbert was also dropped from the team. Their places were taken by Ferrari drivers Gerhard Berger and Jean Alesi, but this effectively saw the team drop down a gear in terms of the intensity and focus of its World Championship challenge.

Berger and Alesi were fine drivers, but there was no way they could be regarded in the same class as Michael Schumacher. No-one could. Two World Championship seasons were now followed by a couple of bleak years during which Benetton would only win a single grand prix.

The Benetton B196 was launched with due ceremony and glitz at Taormina, in Sicily, against the spectacular backdrop of Mount Etna. The team's Technical Director Ross Brawn played his cards very close to his chest prior to the unveiling of the new car which clearly owed much to the machine which had gone before.

Flavio Briatore set himself up for the most almighty fall by grandly announcing at the launch that Benetton was as strong as ever. 'All we have changed is the two drivers,' he proclaimed. Which was, of course, the entire point. In fact the only significant difference was that Benetton had changed one driver. The best in the business.

It was certainly a painful process of transition. Inevitably, the new car inherited some of the 'pointy' front end qualities which Michael Schumacher had so relished. But Berger and Alesi wanted a less nervous machine and Gerhard's frustration was heightened by the fact that he badly damaged one of the B195s in an early test at the end of the 1995 season.

'It is amazing how long it takes for a driver and a team to get used to each other,' said Ross Brawn towards the end of the '96 season. 'When you have two new drivers then it's hardly likely to be any easier. Both Jean and

New generation. Briatore with the two drivers who faced the unenviable task of picking up Schumacher's standard after he moved to Ferrari in 1996, Jean Alesi and Gerhard Berger. (Formula One Pictures)

Hmmm, but what did it feel like exactly? Berger testing the Benetton B196 at Estoril before the start of the 1996 season. (Formula One Pictures)

Gerhard had an approach [after their years together at Ferrari] which was in some ways better and some ways worse than our own. What we had to do was marry the two together. We gradually achieved that, but the first few races of the season were certainly extremely difficult.'

It was hard to ascertain precisely how much of the problem could be attributed to the drivers and how much to the team. Clearly both needed to adapt their approach to each other, coming as they did from widely varied recent racing backgrounds. Should both sides of the partnership have compromised more?

'Probably,' said Brawn reflectively. 'But a good driver has to be prepared to adapt his style, even under normal circumstances. You can never set up a car the same for every race. The driver knows fundamentally what he wants, but there will always be different degrees of success in achieving that.

'For instance, because the tyres change [their characteristics] during a race, the driver might start with a bit of understeer which progresses to oversteer. He's got to be able to cope with that. He has to have the ability to adopt a slightly different style to suit the car.

'On the other hand, our car was too aggressive and over-responsive. All the things that Michael could extract the most from were not suitable for Jean and Gerhard. Any good racing car is consistent because of the confident feed-back from the driver, and we didn't have that. We had to find ways of making the car more predictable and more consistent, enabling the drivers to become accustomed to it and get the maximum out of it.

'I don't think the car we had was quicker for Michael. It was just that he found it acceptable. In actual fact, because of the approach we had to take with the B196, the car that we had towards the end of the season was a better car and Michael himself would have gone a lot quicker in it than he did with the B195.'

The 1996 season began with the Australian Grand Prix at Melbourne, an event which finished on a somewhat uncomfortable note. Alesi and Berger qualified the new Benetton B196s sixth and seventh and, while Gerhard managed a distant fourth, Jean Alesi spun himself into retirement early in the race after hitting Eddie Irvine's Ferrari during an ill-starred overtaking move.

Alesi then entered a promising patch. He finished second to Damon Hill's Williams FW18 at Interlagos, then lost a possible second place at Buenos Aires when he stalled at his final pit stop, eventually finishing third. Berger picked up the Benetton standard and was holding a strong second place with 15 laps of the Argentine GP left to run when he slid off the road due to a broken rear torsion bar.

The Austrian had also mistakenly assumed he was in the lead, misinterpreting a 'FUEL P1' signal – which was

Berger with Benetton team manager Joan Villadelprat at the 1996 Brazilian Grand Prix.
(Formula One Pictures)

recommending he adjust to a leaner engine setting – for a sign that he had taken the lead from Hill. 'That was a big disappointment for me,' said Gerhard after the race. 'I needed a good result, perhaps to remind people that I'm not over the top just yet.'

From then on, it all went wrong. Neither driver showed decent form at the European GP at Nurburgring. As the starting signal was given, both Alesi and Berger crawled away from the line when the 'parking brakes' on their Benettons – activated by press-button controls on the steering wheels and used to prevent creeping on the starting grid – somehow malfunctioned. Berger's right front wheel was locked solid for the first 50 yards.

Alesi was furious. From fourth place on the grid he completed the opening lap in 13th position. It was entirely predictable that the volatile Frenchman's temper would spill over into irrational track behaviour. Sure enough, going into the braking area for the first corner, he launched his Benetton down the inside of Mika Salo's Tyrrell in what, by any standards, was an absurdly optimistic overtaking manoeuvre.

It was never going to work. The two cars collided, plunging into the gravel trap on the outside of the corner, and while Salo was able to keep going, Alesi was out on the spot with broken suspension.

That wasn't the end of it. Alesi was subsequently penalised with a $2,500 fine for running across the circuit and

Briatore looks thoughtful on the pit wall, worrying perhaps about the loss of his star driver. (Formula One Pictures)

Benetton later had to pick up the tab for an additional $10,000 penalty for the Frenchman leaving the circuit without reporting to race control, an obligatory requirement for anybody involved in an accident.

I blame myself, and sometimes the team, not just the drivers

And there was more. Berger completed the opening lap by coming straight into the pits for attention, rightly hoping that his crew would be ready to change tyres. Unfortunately his radio did not appear to be working, with the result that his mechanics were caught on the hop when his B196 appeared at their feet. After some delay, and duly equipped with fresh rubber, he resumed a distant 18th. He finished the race a lapped ninth.

Flavio Briatore was aghast over the way things seemed to be slipping. On the eve of the following race, the San Marino Grand Prix at Imola, the Benetton team chief summoned both his drivers to what was, by all accounts, an absolutely electrifying confrontation in the paddock motorhome. 'It was real blood on the walls stuff,' said one shocked team insider.

In short, he told Alesi and Berger – in addition to the engineering team – that they had to raise the standard of their game, or concede that there was no chance of retaining the World Championship. 'If we fail in the next three races, then we can forget about this season and start building the car for 1997. Anything that happens at Imola has to be better than the last race.

'I never believed it was so difficult when you change some major structure, in this case the two drivers. You face a completely new problem, a new situation, and I blame myself sometimes and sometimes the team, not just the drivers, because we need to modify the system by which we work.

'We are too used to winning with somebody else so it's quite natural to keep working the way we have done for the past five years. But you have to understand that other drivers who have been working with other teams will be in completely different shape.

'On the Thursday at Imola we had a meeting between the team and the drivers – which was very useful – to find out what is the problem. We know that our car is very quick in race trim and we are all very well aware that the race is more important than qualifying, as illustrated by the fact that in 1995 we won 11 races with only two pole positions.'

Berger and Alesi finished third and sixth at Imola. It was an improvement, but far less than the team was expecting. At Monaco, however, Alesi came very close to victory after Damon Hill's Williams retired just beyond half distance.

Jean had been running a strong second up to that point and now went through into a commanding lead. But

Jean Alesi, mercurial, unpredictable talent.
(Formula One Pictures)

Striking a blow for F1 seniors

Gerhard Berger demonstrated that his role as F1's Senior Citizen had in no way blunted his competitive edge when he scored a dominant victory in the 1997 German Grand Prix at Hockenheim.

This circuit had great significance for Berger. It was here that he gave Ferrari their emotional win in 1994, and here that he experienced huge disappointment in 1996 when, just two laps from victory, after parrying Damon Hill's very best efforts, the engine on his Benetton suddenly gave out.

But there was even more to it. This was the 37-year-old Austrian's comeback race after missing three grands prix because of sinus problems. He knew he would not be driving for the team the following year and that Wurz, the young test driver who had stood in for him with such panache, would probably take his place.

There was of course added poignance as the win came less than three weeks after the death of Gerhard's father in a light aircraft accident in the Tirol. Although never one to get mawkish, Gerhard did say at the post-race press conference, 'I felt I had a special power this weekend, and I'm sure I don't need to explain where it came from'.

In any event, there was great rejoicing for this popular driver. Berger finished the race 17.5 sec ahead of Michael Schumacher's Ferrari, the German driver extending his championship advantage to ten points over Silverstone winner Jacques Villeneuve who spun off while running fourth with 12 of the race's 45 laps left to run. Villeneuve's failure to finish rounded off the worst day in recent memory for the Williams team – Benetton's key Renault-engined rivals – after Heinz-Harald Frentzen retired at the end of the opening lap with damaged suspension following a first corner collision with Eddie Irvine's Ferrari.

'I have experienced big emotions throughout the weekend,' said Berger after celebrating on the podium. 'This has been special for me, very special. I have to say I am happy for myself today, but also for the team.

'It really was time to give something back to them. After Michael left at the end of 1995, it was difficult to change to another area, so I am very happy for them all. We have come close several times, but today takes away some of the pressure. I hope I gave them what they deserved.'

Berger said that he had been lucky to finish after Jan Magnussen's Stewart-Ford had blown up its engine in a cloud of smoke right in front of him. 'I thought I had lost the race. I almost had to stop because I could not see. I thought I would not be able to get ahead after my final pit stop, but I was very surprised that I was only just behind Giancarlo Fisichella when I came back into the race.'

He also joked that he had struck a blow for F1's older generation. 'The younger drivers still have to practise a little bit!'

Berger, a veteran of 203 grand prix starts over almost 14 seasons, had been in a class of his own throughout qualifying, taking pole position with exuberant aplomb. He then never looked back as he sped to the tenth victory of his career.

His success – Benetton's first since Schumacher won at Suzuka in 1995 – was regarded as a timely snub to the Briatore who had effectively advised Berger three weeks earlier that Benetton would not be requiring his services in 1998, although they had the good grace to allow him to make the official announcement of his 'decision' to leave. This came only two days after the team announced that it would be taking up its option on Giancarlo Fisichella.

'I will not drive for Benetton in 1998,' said Gerhard, obviously with mixed feelings. 'It is not [a question of] the team or its performance level. I had a personal two year plan when I joined them last year and I will have completed that.

'There are a few things available outside F1 for me, but I just have to see what happens over the next three or four races. I don't want to be a team boss and I am not worried about money at this stage of my career. I want to keep in F1, but it doesn't necessarily have to be with a team that is winning at the moment.'

Nine months later, Gerhard would be appointed BMW Motorsports Director as the German car company began the countdown to its forthcoming engine supply partnership with the Williams team, due to start in the year 2000.

Gerhard Berger on the way to a stunning victory in the 1997 German Grand Prix. (Formula One Pictures)

with only 15 of the race's 75 laps left to run, he crawled into the pits to report badly deteriorating handling. A rear spring had broken and, after another exploratory lap, he was forced to call it a day. Berger, meanwhile, had retired early on with a failed gearbox sensor.

A splendid run to second place behind Schumacher's Ferrari in the rain-soaked Spanish GP at Barcelona boosted Alesi's morale and the Frenchman followed that up with third at Montreal behind the dominant Williams FW18s of Damon Hill and Jacques Villeneuve. The French Grand Prix at Magny-Cours produced third and fourth places for Alesi and Berger behind the Williams duo, rounding off

a Renault-propelled 1–2–3–4 grand slam. Berger followed that up with a strong second at Silverstone where Alesi retired after a seized wheel bearing caused him to spin off.

Then came Hockenheim where Berger, one of the bravest drivers in the business, qualified his Benetton second to join Hill on the front row and then led from the start. Gerhard lost his lead to the Englishman when he had to make his routine refuelling stop, but regained the advantage when Hill made his own stop ten laps later.

From then on it was a flat-out battle with Damon pulling every trick in the book as he attempted to get on terms with the Benetton driver. It looked as

Jean Alesi's Benetton-Renault B196 in the 1996 European GP at Nurburgring, a fiasco of a race for both drivers after their 'parking brakes' jammed on at the start. (Formula One Pictures)

though it might go right down to the wire, yet three laps from the end Gerhard's car suffered a massive engine failure while running only a few yards ahead of his English rival.

'I came out of the Clark curve and suddenly heard one of our engines make a strange noise,' said Hill. 'I thought it might be mine, but Gerhard moved slightly to the left and I dodged through before it erupted.' Hill was thus left with an easy win over Alesi in the second Benetton as Gerhard reflected on his abject disappointment.

'I really looked in good shape and could not believe what happened,' he shrugged. 'Everything was perfect and I was confident that I could have held Hill off as I had done for the previous ten laps. C'est la vie!'

Since the British Grand Prix

Benetton had moved into second place in the Constructors' Championship table. Third place for Alesi in the Hungarian Grand Prix consolidated that position by a margin of 13 points. There was no question of catching the dominant Williams squad, but at least the Benetton lads began to think they might end the season as 'best of the rest.'

However, from here on in, the contest would become nerve-wrackingly close. Schumacher won for Ferrari at both Spa and Monza, but Alesi and Berger were fourth and sixth in the Belgian race, followed by Jean taking second place in the Italian GP. Now the gap was down to three points with only two races to go.

At Estoril in the Portuguese Grand Prix, Schumacher was third with Alesi

and Berger fourth and sixth. Benetton was now just a single point ahead of Ferrari as they went into the final round of the title chase, the Japanese Grand Prix at Suzuka.

Gerhard had won at Suzuka for Ferrari back in 1987 and really liked the spectacular circuit near Nagoya. His B196 worked well there and he qualified fourth, then made a brilliant start to come round second behind Damon Hill's Williams at the end of the opening lap.

Winning the title meant we didn't put enough time into the new car

Gerhard had opted for a three stop strategy and because of this reckoned he could run quicker than Hill. Coming into the tight chicane at the end of lap three, he made a dart up the inside of the Williams, but Damon didn't see him coming. He closed the door and Berger had to steer up the kerb, damaging his car's nose section, as the only means of avoiding a collision.

'I was going faster than Damon,' he explained. 'I was not sure whether he was on a two stop strategy, which is why I thought it was important to try and get ahead and build up a lead, but unfortunately the move did not come off. If Damon said he didn't see me, then I believe him; he is not that sort of driver [to lie].'

Meanwhile, Alesi had managed to write off his own car in a huge accident at the first corner on the opening lap of the race. Berger fought back to take fourth after an unscheduled stop to replace his car's nose section, but Schumacher's Ferrari finished second to Hill. Williams thus clinched the Constructors' title with an astronomic 175 points. Ferrari wound up second on 70 points, Benetton came third just two points behind. Flavio Briatore was not amused.

To be fair, the Benetton B196 had been significantly improved during the course of the season. 'By the time we got to Spa at the end of August, we were beginning to see the light at the end of the tunnel,' reflected Ross Brawn.

'We were working better as a team. There were a lot of things which needed to be considered and, for the drivers, it went deeper than simply what they did at the wheel. They needed to look at the team's engineering approach and understand why things were done in a certain way.

'Everything has to come together. I think it was at Hockenheim that I said to Gerhard and Jean that, if we could have been in that position at the beginning of the season, imagine how much more positive we would have felt.

'I think anyone who has won a Championship will tell you that it takes an awful lot out of the team because you work hard right up to the end of the year. The 1995 Championship was pretty tight for most of the season and it meant we didn't put as much time as we would have liked into the new car.

'This season we made an extra-

Jean Alesi gives Gerhard Berger a lift home at Hockenheim after the Austrian driver's engine failed a couple of laps from victory in the 1996 German Grand Prix. (Formula One Pictures)

special effort so that the 1997 car would be started early in order to give us plenty of time to consider all the options. We've made a lot of progress and are working much better with the drivers. We intended to start Melbourne in 1997 at least as strong as we were in our better races in 1996. Overall, the '96 season was a disappointment, but, as always, you learn from these things.'

By the end of the season, Brawn decided to do some personal stock taking. He enjoyed his time with Benetton, but had been really stimulated during the Michael Schumacher years. Now came an offer to join Ferrari as Technical Director. It was a challenge he could not ignore, so he decided to follow Michael's example

and leave Benetton, albeit a year behind the German driver.

This now gave Pat Symonds the opportunity to move forward and take over the task of Technical Director with Nick Wirth, the former Simtek F1 team chief who joined Benetton to take charge of R&D, moving into the role of Chief Designer. The experienced Joan Villadelprat continued his position as Team Manager, so the consequences of Ross Brawn's departure – soon to be followed by Rory Byrne – were minimised.

True to Brawn's predictions, the new Benetton B197 was ready early, in fact being completed before Christmas 1996 in time for some shakedown tests before its official unveiling the following month. With characteristic

Briatore-style theatricals, the new car was launched at London's Planet Hollywood restaurant amid scenes of hyped-up media chaos by IT girl Tania Bryer all togged up in Benetton team overalls.

Briatore was his customary upbeat self, predicting that Berger and Alesi could realistically expect to be battling with McLaren behind Michael Schumacher's Ferrari and the Williams team for third place in the coming season's F1 pecking order.

We were quickest in the test and have put many miles on the car

---

That was the candid prediction from the Italian team chief a month after the B197 first broke cover at Silverstone and fresh from Berger's quickest testing time the previous week at Jerez. It might have seemed an almost painfully frank assessment of Benetton's potential, but Briatore always shot from the hip. 'Ferrari is strong, Michael Schumacher we know is the best driver and after that I would expect Williams to be there as usual,' he said.

Despite this, Berger and Alesi indicated they would be out to prove that the B197, produced by the new design team directed by Symonds and Wirth, could be a Championship contender. The emphasis had been on an evolutionary development of the previous year's car which both drivers had diffi-

culty handling. With subtly revised aerodynamics and suspension detailing, first signs for the B197 during the Jerez test looked extremely promising.

Symonds admitted that it was necessary to undergo a process of mental recalibration when it came to the design work. 'Losing Michael was a major disappointment,' he said. 'In retrospect we had under-estimated the effect of the discontinuity. Because we'd worked with Michael over many years, we'd forgotten what it took to get settled in with a new driver. I think we realised that very early on; it takes a while to get to know your drivers, to get to know what's wanted.

'That procedure carried throughout last year, but you get to the point where you've gone as far as you can with a design and you've got your ideas for the next one. So this car (B197) is very much tailored to the 1996/97 drivers.'

Symonds said that there were some very specific areas of the B196 design which had needed addressing when it came to the new car, throw-backs to the pointy, oversteering set-up which Schumacher favoured.

'I don't really want to go into details of what they were, but there were limitations we'd reached in the design,' he said. 'You tend to evolve your set-ups towards a driver, and then you find you've reached the end of the road and you need to take the design more in that direction rather than the set-up.'

The new Benetton owed much of its concept to Symonds's longtime colleague Rory Byrne. It featured double wishbone/pushrod suspension all round with twin dampers at the rear and the facility for a triple damper set-

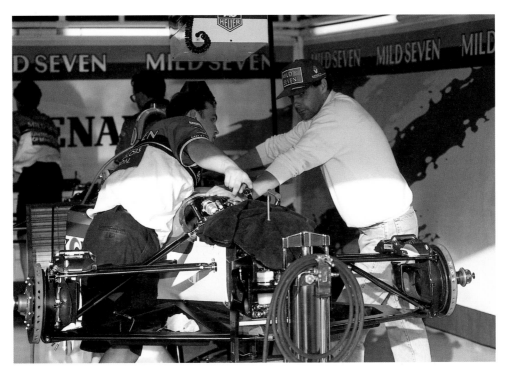

Berger in discussion at the 1997 Brazilian Grand Prix where he finished a morale-boosting second to Jacques Villeneuve's Williams. (Formula One Pictures)

up at the front, while Symonds had replaced the previous year's seven-speed gearbox with a six-speed unit for reasons of reduced weight and improved packaging. As far as the new Benetton's engine package was concerned, although Renault was still committed to pulling out of F1 at the end of the 1997 season, Bernard Dudot's design team at Renault Sport was determined to sustain its competitive edge for its clients Benetton and Williams right through to the final race of the year.

Hence the advent of the all-new RS9 V10 with a 71-degree vee angle – four degrees wider than the previous year's RS8 – which was also 11kg lighter than its predecessor and 14mm lower. Now capable of running at almost 17,000rpm, the new engine was tipped to produce an extra 10bhp, taking its output to around 740bhp.

Yet Briatore seemed strangely keen to keep Benetton's aspirations under control, perhaps mindful that his pre-season predictions in 1996 had been embarrassingly wide of the mark. 'Ferrari has the edge, technically and economically. They have done a lot of shopping for key staff,' he said, referring to Brawn's recent defection there. 'But we must work hard to get on terms with them. They have the best driver, but I expect we will perform much better than we did last season.'

Gerhard Berger comments at the launch were cautiously optimistic. 'It is always difficult to make an accurate judgement at this stage of the year. We were quickest in the test, but an even better sign is that we have put many miles on the cars without any problems. The new engine feels as though it has more top-end power.' Both drivers felt highly motivated.

Berger opened the season on an upbeat note with fourth place at Melbourne followed by a vigorous chase into second place just 4.19 sec behind Villeneuve's Williams FW19 at Interlagos. By contrast, Alesi kicked off his programme with a bizarre lapse in Australia, running his B197's tank dry after 34 laps of the 58-lap circuit having repeatedly ignored signals to come in for fuel and tyres.

It was terrible to waste the race for such a silly reason

Jean had seemed totally immersed in his battle with Mika Hakkinen's McLaren for third place. Despite Nick Wirth literally being hung over the pit walls by his legs in a final attempt to attract his attention, Jean pressed on into lap 35 only to roll to a halt out on the circuit.

'I am obviously extremely disappointed,' he said afterwards in a mood which fluttered between anger and disbelief. 'I had a very good start and was having a very good race. I lost radio contact with the team and did not realise it was time for me to come into the pits for refuelling. I came to a stop, and it was a terrible feeling to

waste the race for such a silly reason.'

When Briatore remarked 'It's a pity for Jean' he must have been feeling much the same. The incident was not calculated to provoke the most sympathetic response and the day ended with Alesi close to tears after a sharp bawling out from his employer. To many observers, this was the start of a slippery slope in terms of the personal relationship between the two men.

In Brazil Alesi was sixth. In Buenos Aires, neither Benetton driver could get the best from their tyres in qualifying and lined up eleventh (Alesi) and twelfth on the grid (Berger). But in the race, Gerhard stormed through to a strong sixth and fastest lap, much encouraged by the feel of the B197 in race set-up.

Berger had lost time when he ran wide avoiding a first corner pile-up and thereafter settled down to claw back some ground. 'This was the hardest race so far this season,' he admitted. 'I tried to keep a steady pace and take out the pressure, always thinking that it was important for me to try and get one or two points. My fastest lap proves once again that the car is competitive, but we obviously have a problem in qualifying and have to work hard in that direction.'

For Alesi, seventh place seemed a poor reward after a race in which he had produced a self-inflicted wound when he tried to pass Damon Hill's Arrows on the outside going into the first right-hander after the pits. Both cars spun as a result, losing valuable time.

And so the year unfolded. The B197 settled down to produce a consistent

Courted by two major teams

Having decided that Giancarlo Fisichella should be one of its drivers in 1998, Benetton then found itself having to launch a legal battle with Jordan to adjudicate which team was entitled to the 24-year-old Italian's services. In September, Benetton won an action in London's High Court to establish that Eddie Jordan would

Giancarlo Fisichella, a World Champion in the making? (Formula One Pictures)

indeed have to relinquish his own claim. After a two day hearing Mr Justice Jacob found in favour of Benetton who had originally loaned Fisichella to Jordan for 1997. He ordered that Jordan should write to the FIA's Contract Recognition Board advising them that Fisichella would be driving for Benetton the following season.

Fisichella had been loaned to Jordan at the start of 1997 because Benetton already had existing driver contracts with Jean Alesi and Gerhard Berger through until the end of the season. But only until then. This youngster was hot property.

Fisichella – who had achieved considerable success in Italian F3 and the International and German Touring Car Championships – moved up to F1 in 1996, driving eight races for Minardi before impressing Benetton with his speed and confidence in a test at Estoril.

The idea of 'placing' Fisichella with Jordan – who were also paid a reputed $1 million dollar (£670,000) fee to accommodate him – was always with a view to the driver returning to Benetton at the end of the year. Benetton said this was clear from the outset, but admitted that Fisichella had to negotiate his own driving contract with Jordan, believed to be a modest $100,000 dollars (£65,000).

The High Court decision came as a major blow for Jordan. The Silverstone team – still striving for its maiden victory – had held out great hopes for the Italian who finished second in the Belgian Grand Prix, third in Canada, and fourth at both Imola and in front of his home crowd at Monza ten days prior to the court hearing. But Jordan's loss was Benetton's gain, as would be demonstrated in 1998.

sequence of top six results, but only a single win when Gerhard Berger delivered an outstanding performance to triumph in the German Grand Prix at Hockenheim. Apart from that, 1997 could best be remembered as a season of close calls and near misses.

Berger also missed several races with serious sinus problems which resulted in test driver Alexander Wurz being promoted to the race team for the Canadian, French and British Grands Prix.

In qualifying where tyres get hammered, we have a problem

The lanky Wurz, who started his competitive life racing BMW bicycles around Europe, not only proved an adept and intelligent test driver but also drove very competently on those three race outings. The highlight was Silverstone where he shadowed Jean Alesi home to a Benetton 2–3 behind winner Jacques Villeneuve.

Wurz was clearly a man with an F1 future and it was as well for Berger's reputation that his comeback race at Hockenheim should have produced such an outstanding win. Nevertheless, with Giancarlo Fisichella – on 'loan' to Jordan – clearly targeted by Briatore as a driver for the Benetton team in 1998, it hardly required a clairvoyant to see that Wurz was now strong favourite for the second drive. In other words, whatever they might achieve in the second half of

the 1997 season, Berger and Alesi were not going to have their contracts renewed for the following year.

Even so, the general consensus at Benetton was that the B197 made a degree of progress in the second half of the year. 'I know we've had our ups and downs,' explained Pat Symonds, 'but this year's chassis has certainly been a machine which the drivers preferred to last year's. With the possible exception of Austria, I think the problems were very much down to how we could make the tyres work on the low grip circuits.

'With that exception, when we could get the car onto a circuit where we could get some load into it, then we could make the tyres work. Unfortunately many of our problems arose at the early circuits – Melbourne, Buenos Aires, Imola and Monaco – all circuits we can't test at, the ones where it is very difficult to get the car loaded up and the tyres utilised properly.

'This has been our problem with our cars for a considerable amount of time. I think you've only got to look back to 1994/95 with Michael when we were winning an awful lot of races, but we didn't actually get so many pole positions. Our qualifying wasn't as good as our racing. I would say that our design philosophy over the years has evolved in a way that we make a car which is very kind to its tyres. So in a race, it is a good package. But in qualifying, when the tyres need to be used more vigorously, there has been a problem.'

Jean Alesi's Benetton B197 on its way to fifth place in the 1997 French Grand Prix. (Formula One Pictures)

Nevertheless, Symonds believed that the team had started to get some clues as to how to handle this tyre temperature issue to the benefit of future Benetton designs. 'If I could spend a week testing at Melbourne or Buenos Aires, I think we could learn a bit more about our problem,' he said. 'But that's basically the reason behind our ups and downs.'

Of the team's two regular drivers, Alesi was the most consistent. Second places in the Canadian, British, Italian and Luxembourg Grands Prix helped boost his points total until he was challenging Frentzen for third place in the drivers' table going into the final race of the season.

Jean also gained the second pole position of his career at Monza, leading commandingly in the opening stages of the race only to be leapfrogged by Coulthard's McLaren at the refuelling stop, as the team expected. With a bigger fuel tank than the Benetton, Coulthard was able to start with more fuel and therefore needed to take on less when he made his stop. The McLaren's advantage was almost preordained, in that respect, reflects Symonds. Not that this made it any less frustrating for the team!

Yet it was Berger's victory at Hockenheim which really propelled Benetton into the headlines. Starting from pole, Gerhard's B197 was abso-

lutely the class of the field from start to finish. However this was a rare high moment for the Austrian who retired from racing at the end of a season bedevilled by the sinus problems, not to mention having to cope with the tragic death of his father.

'When you look back on the season, Jean had brought in quite a lot of points for Benetton,' summed up Symonds in 1997. 'He keeps bringing in the prizes and, this year, he has driven some really rather good races. In Barcelona and Canada, for example, he quickly sorted out how to get the best out of the tyres and at Monza, of course, he was battling against that fundamental problem posed by the

McLaren. I think he did a good, consistent job.

'As for Gerhard, he suffered from his health problems an awful lot more than people have realised. It's a matter of history that he had those three races off, but maybe it should have happened earlier, because I think he was suffering quite badly from Argentina onwards without anybody – himself included – quite realising how much it was taking out of him.

'That ruined what was potentially a fantastic season for Gerhard. After the pre-season testing I thought "wow, the guy has got a new lease of life" and would be pretty successful. I don't think he showed his full potential until he came back at Hockenheim. It was a great shame. If you took away that health problem, he had every chance of retiring on a very high note, and I just wish he could have done.'

Symonds and the Benetton engineering team seemed almost self-conscious in their assertion that 1997 was generally disappointing, although on paper it certainly looked rather better than that.

With the colourful Flavio Briatore bowing out of F1 at the end of the season, his place taken over by Prodrive boss David Richards, the powerhouse behind Subaru's World Rally Championship success, Benetton was now confident of opening a new phase in its history. What followed next was a big push to get back up alongside Williams and Ferrari for 1998.

Chapter 4

New generation

With the departure of Gerhard Berger and Jean Alesi, Benetton went into the 1998 World Championship battle with its fortunes resting squarely on the shoulders of two promising young guns, Giancarlo Fisichella and Alexander Wurz. On the strength of what we had seen from both of them in 1997, Benetton were set to benefit from their gusto and commitment.

By the same token, they formed a dramatic contrast to the seasoned Berger/Alesi partnership. Did new Benetton boss David Richards feel slightly concerned that his driver line-up lacked the strength and experience that some people felt the team might need at this point in its history?

Quite the reverse. Although Richards had only come in on the tail end of the partnership, it was clear that the relationship between these two former Ferrari drivers and the Benetton team had run its course.

Richards found them both person-ally charming, but admits he could detect rumblings of discontent from the factory floor. Those who worked with the drivers, and on the cars, found them over-demanding and fussy to the point of irritation, a situation exacerbated by the fact that, with the glorious exception of Berger's Hockenheim performance, they fell short on delivering the required results.

Admittedly it had not been easy for Alesi and Berger. Michael Schumacher was always going to be a hard act to follow. Between 1992 and 1995, Benetton had developed an appetite for race victories. To have scored only a single triumph over the following two seasons was frustrating and acutely disappointing.

Facing the 1998 season with Fisichella and Wurz on the team's books suffused everybody with enor-

United front. Giancarlo Fisichella (left) and Alexander Wurz, 1998. (Formula One Pictures)

mous optimism. Just as Alesi and Berger had sometimes seemed like soldiers suffering from battle fatigue, the youngsters shone with vigour. It was just the tonic Benetton needed.

'It is always something of a gamble having new drivers on the team, no matter how sure you might be about what they have to offer,' admitted Richards. 'There is no doubt that they both have the talent and sometimes the sheer enthusiasm and commitment radiated by younger drivers has a beneficial effect. It rubs off on everyone around them, inspiring everybody's efforts.

'At the same time, one tends to be more tolerant of any mistakes a young driver might make in circumstances where you might be slightly annoyed if a more experienced hand did the same. The only potential snag I see is the fact that we've got two new drivers at the same time. Ideally there should always be a degree of overlap and I am currently reviewing the contract situation to make sure that this happens in the future.'

On the subject of Oliver Gavin's possible role as test driver, Richards said that he'd seen little of the Englishman on the track. 'There's no commitment between us yet because frankly I think the role of a test driver in 1998 will be less than before. As Giancarlo and Alexander are young and relatively new to it, I think they will want all the testing miles they can get.'

The 1998 season inevitably produced

1998 Australian GP. New season, new hopes. (ICN UK Bureau)

a huge challenge with the introduction of new F1 technical regulations requiring much narrower cars producing less aerodynamic downforce, plus grooved tyres from manufacturers Goodyear and Bridgestone. Goodyear, of course, had been Benetton's long-time tyre supplier and the team had a contract in place with the US corporation through to the

end of the 1999 season.

However, during 1997, Goodyear's senior management concluded that F1 had served its purpose as a crucible for technical development and it was now time to deploy its financial resources elsewhere. With that in mind, it formally announced that it would be withdrawing from grand prix racing at the end of the 1998 season subject, of course, to any subsequent corporate change of mind.

Clearly Goodyear was not going to be in a position to fulfil the terms of its Benetton contract, so it was no surprise when Richards promptly arranged a switch to Bridgestone, one year in advance of a possible scenario which

could see that company as F1's sole tyre supplier.

Richards felt it was the only way forward. 'We need to be associated with companies and technical partners who have the same level of intensity when it comes to their commitment.' His decision to move did not exactly delight McLaren chief Ron Dennis whose new MP4/13 challengers were now running on Bridgestone rubber after making a similar switch a few months ahead of the Benetton squad.

Wurz, made of strong stuff, was not fazed by Irvine's tactics

Meanwhile, behind the scenes, the development proceeded on the new B198 contender. Benetton Chief Designer Nick Wirth and Technical Director Pat Symonds opted for distinctive short side pods for the new car with additional side impact resistance afforded by aerodynamic deflectors alongside the cockpit.

The team would continue to use Renault-designed V10 engines which were now being commercially marketed under the Mecachrome banner following Renault Sport's withdrawal from F1 at the end of 1997. That withdrawal had the effect of leaving both Williams and Benetton paying £13 million lease fees for the use of these engines – a dramatic contrast to their previous position as works Renault standard bearers – and

Benetton decided to identify its engines under the Playlife brand name, this being one of Benetton's key sports goods marketing brands.

The team went to the opening race in Melbourne feeling guardedly confident. During qualifying at the Albert Park circuit, Giancarlo Fisichella found that the slight increase in ambient temperature during qualifying adversely affected the handling balance of his B198, leaving him battling excessive oversteer. He wound up qualifying seventh, four places ahead of Alexander Wurz who spun off and then took over the race car set up for his team-mate.

Come the race, Fisichella was obliged to take the spare B198 after cracking the steering rack bulkhead on his race car when he spun during the race morning warm-up. This change of machinery certainly didn't inhibit the gusto with which he snapped at Villeneuve's tail and, while many observers believed that his two stop strategy should have enabled him to get ahead of the World Champion, Richards was quick to defend the young Italian. 'You've got to remember that Jacques is a pretty tenacious guy,' he noted.

In the end, Giancarlo retired when a rear wing mount began to crack after 43 laps, leaving Wurz to finish a lapped seventh. It was a rather disappointing start.

On Sao Paulo's bumpy Interlagos circuit, Alexander Wurz qualified fifth to split the two Ferraris of Michael Schumacher and Eddie Irvine on the starting grid.

The quietly confident Austrian was

Wurz preparing to leave the pit garage during practice for the 1998 Brazilian Grand Prix.
(Formula One Pictures)

well pleased with his efforts, although Fisichella spun during what he reckoned was a very quick lap and had to run back to the pits to take the spare car. He qualified seventh. 'Unfortunately the spare car was set up for Alex, so I was not able to improve in the last few minutes,' he explained.

Come the race, Wurz – in only his fifth grand prix – drove superbly, running a one stop strategy which kept him out very late during the race in an effort to maximise his strategic possibilities. The McLaren-Mercedes were again in a class of their own, but on lap 54 of the 72 lap race, when Schumacher made his second refuelling stop, Maranello fans' hearts leapt into their mouths as the Ferrari engine briefly stalled, keeping the car at rest for an agonising 13.1sec.

This dropped Michael from third to fourth place behind Irvine, but he managed to squeeze back into the race ahead of the impressive Wurz who had just outbraked Frentzen into the left-hander after the pits in what was, by common consensus, the overtaking move of the race.

'I enjoyed that,' said Wurz, who had made his sole refuelling stop on lap 46. 'I had a long first stint, and the tyres went off towards the end, so Michael pushed me hard, but I could stay ahead because I had less fuel in the car and I could brake a little later.' He finished fourth while Fisichella wound up sixth, one lap down.

Two weeks later, Wurz again impressed with his performance in the Argentine GP at Buenos Aires. The Austrian drove extremely well, his

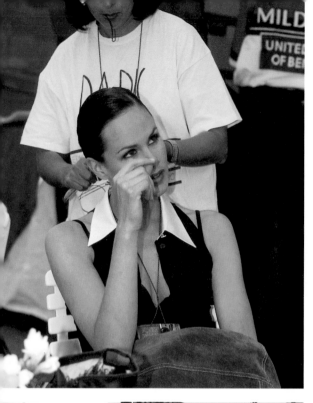

Glamour is part of the grand prix game.
(Formula One Pictures)

Bridgestone-shod B198 running a one stop strategy with a long opening stint which kept him out until the end of lap 40 by which time he was running fourth. He lost only a single place and moved back to fourth place when Alesi made his second stop at the end of lap 50.

After Eddie Irvine came in at the end of lap 55, Wurz was in striking distance of the Ferrari. Getting past would clearly be quite another matter, but the young Austrian is made of strong stuff and wasn't put off in the slightest when Irvine chopped across him on lap 59 and the two cars made quite heavy contact.

What did he expect me to do – go into helicopter mode?

The Benetton driver eventually elbowed his way past Irvine on lap 64, only to spin three laps later and drop back behind the Ferrari for the remainder of the race, finishing fourth. 'I made a mistake,' shrugged Wurz, 'although after I collided with Irvine the car became a little more difficult to drive.' Fisichella wound up a slightly disappointed seventh.

The Benetton team followed that up with a troubled run on its home turf at Imola in the San Marino GP, although Wurz again out-qualified Fisichella, lining up fifth – five places ahead of the Italian who just couldn't get the car running to his taste. Unfortunately, at the start, the steering wheel gearchange mechanism on Wurz's car went haywire and he was nudged from behind by Damon Hill's Jordan on the sprint to the first corner, thankfully without the Benetton suffering any damage. Nevertheless, Alex had to come in at the end of the opening lap for a replacement steering wheel to be fitted and he resumed right at the tail of the field.

Meanwhile, with 15 laps of the race run, Fisichella was getting really energetic in his pursuit of Frentzen's ill-handling Williams, darting around on the tail of the German's car and looking for any overtaking opportunity which might present itself.

On lap 18 Fisichella got a little too close to the Williams going into the Villeneuve chicane, lost control and spun heavily into the wall. The Benetton was quite badly rumpled in the impact and, as if that wasn't enough for the team, Wurz retired next time round with gearbox failure, having been lapped by the leaders following his earlier delay. It was hardly a day to savour.

The Spanish GP at Barcelona might well have yielded a podium finish for Fisichella, who qualified fourth, one place ahead of Wurz on this occasion. It was a morale-boosting performance by the Italian who had been quite uncomfortably bruised in the accident at Imola and followed that up by crashing again during pre-race testing at the Circuit de Catalunya.

But Fisichella found himself embroiled in a tactical battle with Ferrari number two Eddie Irvine, the Ulsterman slowing the pace in an

Wurz ahead of Fisichella as the two Benettons queue to leave the pit lane at the start of practice for the 1998 Canadian Grand Prix. (Formula One Pictures)

effort to help vault the slow-starting Michael Schumacher ahead of both himself and the Benetton driver at his first refuelling stop.

Eddie had taken an immediate third place ahead of Fisichella at the start, but after his first refuelling stop he slowed his pace by three seconds in one lap under team orders, thereby allowing Schumacher to return to the circuit ahead, having made up two places.

Fisichella, who now found himself back in fifth place, then attempted to overtake Irvine round the outside of the first corner at the start of lap 29, the two cars colliding and spinning into retirement in the gravel trap.

Fisichella remonstrated energetically with Irvine as the two men walked away from their abandoned cars, but the stewards eventually decided that the fault lay with the Italian who was fined $7500 for 'causing an avoidable accident.' Many people regarded this as a very harsh judgement.

Irvine was characteristically direct about the episode. 'He just came down the outside and turned into me, taking the racing line despite the fact I was there. What did he expect me to do? Press a button and go into immediate helicopter mode?'

Fisichella clearly didn't think that was an explanation which warranted a great deal of credibility. 'I am very disappointed,' he admitted. 'I had already passed Irvine with most of the car and he should have let me through, but he kept on going and it resulted in a collision.

'At the beginning of the race the

same thing occurred, but I was on the inside and I pulled back to let Eddie through as I knew it would end in an accident. Apart from the collision, after a few laps the car became difficult to drive with both understeer and oversteer, but I was in a strong position for third place.'

Wurz salvaged the day with fourth place in Spain, but two weeks later both Benetton drivers were right on the pace when it came to the most prestigious race on the calendar, the Monaco GP through the streets of Monte Carlo.

Both drivers gave dazzling displays of controlled aggression

Mika Hakkinen absolutely dominated the race for the McLaren-Mercedes team, but Michael Schumacher's efforts to shine for Ferrari were badly undermined by the intervention of both Benetton drivers who produced dazzling displays of controlled aggression in these very demanding surroundings.

Hakkinen took the chequered flag 11.4 sec ahead of the impressive Fisichella who drove his B198 with great aplomb, despite a harmless spin, to beat Eddie Irvine's Ferrari into third place by more than half a minute.

Starting from pole position, Hakkinen just managed to squeeze out his team-mate David Coulthard on the crucial 300-metre sprint to Ste Devote,

the tricky off-camber right-hander which leads up the hill towards Casino Square. Thereafter he never looked back, trading fastest laps with his team-mate until Coulthard's engine blew up suddenly and comprehensively midway round the 18th lap.

As if that was not enough, Hakkinen then received a double bonus when Michael Schumacher, his only other serious challenger for the world title, produced an uncharacteristically erratic performance which ended on lap 30 when he got involved in a vigorous barging match with Wurz's Benetton as they battled for second place.

As they lapped a group of slower cars, Schumacher dived for the inside line under braking for the first-gear Loews hairpin, but Wurz had no intention of being intimidated into giving way, stayed with the Ferrari on the outside line and then cheekily repassed into the next right-hander.

Schumacher was clearly caught off-balance by this precocity and barged back inside the Benetton to take second place as they accelerated out onto the waterfront. Unfortunately, as he did so, he hit Wurz quite hard, bending a left rear suspension link on the Ferrari which immediately forced him into the pits.

After an initial inspection, Schumacher's reaction was to climb out of the cockpit. However Ross Brawn, the team's Technical Director, instructed him to get back in immedi-

Ready for action. Fisichella prior to the start of the 1998 French Grand Prix. (Formula One Pictures)

ately and refasten his belts while the mechanics worked methodically to repair the damage. Hakkinen had lapped him three times by the time the Ferrari driver accelerated back into the race, now firmly in last position and with very little hope of making up for lost time.

Meanwhile Wurz came in for his refuelling stop at the end of lap 42, resuming third behind team-mate Fisichella only to crash at high speed next time round through the tunnel. The Benetton team confirmed that the accident was caused by damage sustained in the brush with Schumacher. Either way, he was lucky to escape harm in his 170mph impact against the barrier.

At the Canadian Grand Prix, next on the 1998 schedule, both Benetton drivers made the headlines. Fisichella had a great day, actually leading the race for a time as he battled to get on terms with Michael Schumacher's winning Ferrari, but for Wurz the publicity was thanks to another unwelcome accident.

The race began on a nerve-jangling note after Ralf Schumacher stalled his Jordan-Honda from fifth place on the grid. Cars dodged in all directions to avoid the stationary machine with the result that the second half of the grid was well scrambled as it funnelled into the tight left-hander after the pits.

Wurz's Benetton attempted to outbrake Jean Alesi's Sauber going into this turn, and clipped the front of the Swiss car as Alesi moved over to make room for Heinz-Harald Frentzen's Williams to take the racing line.

In a flash, Wurz found himself launched into a horrendous series of somersaults, his car happily landing on its wheels in the gravel trap on the outside of the corner. Alesi, his Sauber team-mate Johnny Herbert and the Prost of Jarno Trulli were also involved and red flags were duly waved all round the circuit to bring the race to a premature halt as Coulthard led Hakkinen round what he was disappointed to discover was not the opening lap of the race.

As the race had not run more than two laps the grid lined up again to compete over the original 69 lap distance. For the restart, Alesi took the spare Sauber, Wurz the spare Benetton and Trulli the spare Prost. Herbert's Sauber was returned to the team garage, repaired and duly joined the restarted race from the pit lane.

This certainly was not Alesi's day for at the restart Ralf Schumacher barged past going into the first corner, spinning in the middle of the pack and again scattering cars in all directions. This ended with Trulli's Prost ending up perched over the back of Alesi's Sauber.

In the middle of all this, Hakkinen suddenly slowed and trailed round at the tail of the field to retire at the end of the opening lap with gearbox trouble. Unfortunately the World Championship points leader was not given the chance to switch to the spare car as this time there was no red flag, the field simply forming up in an orderly queue behind the safety car driven by former British F3 champion – and hopeful candidate for a Benetton test driving role – Oliver Gavin.

When the pack was finally

unleashed at the end of lap five, Coulthard and Schumacher began pulling relentlessly away from the field, Fisichella holding third place ahead of the Williamses of Villeneuve and Frentzen. Schumacher was pressing the Scot extremely hard, occasionally locking up his front tyres under hard braking as he worked away to provoke Coulthard into a slight mistake.

On lap 19 Coulthard suddenly slowed and the second McLaren trailed gently round to the pits to retire with an engine problem, allowing Schumacher through into the lead. Amazingly Gavin had to bring the safety car out again on laps 21 and 22 while debris from Mika Salo's crashed Arrows was cleared up, Schumacher using this lull to make his first refuelling stop.

What happened next was pure farce. As Schumacher emerged from the pits, Frentzen drew level on the outside racing line, but the Ferrari driver simply moved out to the right and pushed him off the circuit and into the gravel trap, an astonishing display of reckless driving.

This left Fisichella's Benetton leading from Villeneuve who, next time round, promptly lunged across the same gravel trap which had claimed Frentzen. He just managed to get back on the track only to be hit from behind by Esteban Tuero's Minardi, resulting in the local hero spending four laps in the pits having the Williams rear wing replaced.

Schumacher now found himself chasing Fisichella for the lead, but had to come in for a 10 sec stop-go penalty, his punishment for the treatment meted out to Frentzen, at the end of lap 35. That put Fisichella ahead again, but Schumacher returned to the lead when the Benetton made its refuelling stop at the end of lap 44. Wurz finished fourth.

This has to have been the craziest race of my career!

'Two second places in two races is an incredible result,' said the delighted Giancarlo after the race. 'I had a big problem at the beginning of the race because I was only doing one pit stop and had a lot of fuel in the car. For the first 15 laps or so there was a lot of understeer and I also had problems with third gear; the gears got stuck when I was changing up, and this got worse as the race went on. But I am delighted with second place.'

Meanwhile, Wurz was behaving with remarkable stoicism, having shrugged aside the effects of that first corner shunt. 'This has to be the craziest race of my career,' he smiled. 'On the first start I was pushed to the left by a Jordan and I touched Alesi's car. It wasn't very hard, but it was enough to make me fly over into the gravel.

'I immediately went on the radio to say I was OK and asked if I could use the T-car for the restart. The race was very hard because with the safety car coming out so many times, it was difficult to keep the tyres at the right temperature. My brakes were also fading, so I needed to concentrate on

Formula 1 is a team game with every player carrying considerable responsibility. (Formula One Pictures)

finishing the race and I could not push Irvine hard as a result. But taken as a whole it is a great result for the team.'

I was happy to have survived – it was pretty scary at times

The unpredictable nature of F1 continued through the French and British Grands Prix where the Benetton B198s had a difficult time. Both were off the pace at Magny-Cours, although Wurz managed to take fifth place, and the two drivers finished fourth (Wurz) and fifth (Fisichella) at Silverstone in a British Grand Prix made chaotic by heavy rain and frustrated for Benetton by the fact that a new Bridgestone tyre – better suited to the McLarens – did not seem to work well on the B198s.

Fisichella and Wurz qualified 11th and 12th, but they performed splendidly in the treacherous race conditions, profiting by the mistakes of others and both running a two stop strategy – the first stint on intermediate rubber and the last two sections on full wets.

'I am really happy with fourth place under the circumstances,' said Wurz. 'I am happy to have survived, because it was pretty scary at times. I think the race probably could have been stopped because of the rain, but we made the right choice and it all went well for me.'

Fisichella added that Alex deserved to finish ahead of him. 'Alex let me by when I was faster,' he recalled, 'then at the end, when he was close behind me, I let him retake the position which was rightfully his. It was fair and worked well for both of us.'

The Benetton team thus finished the Silverstone weekend having consolidated third place in the Constructors' Championship. It was just over halfway through the season and things were looking good.

The team's Mecachrome engine contract – now re-negotiated with the new Supertec Engineering organisation, ironically fronted by Flavio Briatore! – was confirmed for another two years to the end of 2001, although it was no secret that Benetton was looking for a new works engine deal in the longer term.

Characteristically, David Richards was giving absolutely nothing away. 'We are always on the look-out for any beneficial commercial partnerships in the future,' he noted. 'There is obviously a benefit in terms of continuity working with our existing engine supplier, but there is no denying that an exclusive factory-backed programme is preferable.'

In other words, wait, watch and listen. In the meantime, Giancarlo Fisichella and Alexander Wurz continued working hard to put Benetton back where everybody felt that the team belonged. Namely in the winning frame.

Chapter 5

The technical base

Benetton's state-of-the-art technical centre at Enstone provides the engineering heart of the team. Technical Director Pat Symonds and Chief Designer Nick Wirth preside over a committed team of specialists all dedicated to the challenge of producing the best grand prix car design possible.

Symonds has a multi-discipline background which has been perfect for his current role. After studying mechanical engineering in London he got a master's degree in automotive engineering at Cranfield Institute of Technology, then worked as a racing car designer for Hawke and Royale before moving to Toleman in 1981 (where he was race engineer for Ayrton Senna in his maiden F1 season).

For four years he was also Michael Schumacher's race engineer at Benetton and, by all accounts, his authoritative, calm and measured management approach has helped make the Benetton design department a logical, congenial environment in which to work.

Symonds and Wirth collaborate closely on all aspects of Benetton F1 car design.

For his part, 32-year old Wirth previously ran his own F1 team Simtek, which raced through 1993 and 1994, before suffering a crushing body blow when its rookie driver Roland Ratzenberger was killed in practice for the catastrophic 1994 San Marino GP which also saw Ayrton Senna killed while leading the race. Simtek ceased trading the following year and went into liquidation.

It was a painful experience for Wirth who'd been widely regarded as one of the sport's technical high fliers ever since he emerged from University College, London, in 1987 with a first class honours degree in mechanical engineering – and the prize for the best final year thesis, 'Race engine in cylinder flow'.

He worked as senior aerodynamicist for the Leyton House March F1 team, then in 1989 formed Simtek, initially as a motorsport design, research and development service. In 1995 he moved to Benetton as Special Projects Engineer.

'The sort of structure we have at Benetton is that overall responsibility for engineering comes under me,' explains Pat Symonds. 'That includes design, aerodynamics, research and development and electronics. Although not in terms of management of the personnel, it also involves the testing and racing and making fundamental decisions there. In each one of those areas we basically have a head of department.

'In the design office, Nick Wirth obviously takes overall control as Chief Designer, but we also sub-divide it up further. We have a Design Office Manager who is responsible for the scheduling, and then in the main design areas – transmission, mechanical design, composite design – we have section leaders who may, in turn, be responsible for six or seven designers, depending on the department.'

Symonds says he tries to take an overall watching brief. 'I'm not going to look at the detail of how something is designed, that's Nick's job. But it is my job to ensure that we're not designing something we cannot afford to build, or we cannot build in time, that we assign our development priorities correctly and that the different departments are working together properly.

'It is sometimes easy to forget that, in developing a modern F1 car, we need,

Headquarters of the Benetton Formula team is Whiteways Technical Centre, in the Oxfordshire countryside near Chipping Norton. (Benetton)

for example, to integrate mechanical design with electronics. So you have to have a proper project plan and have defined when things are going to be ready, so you don't end up with a load of mechanical parts all waiting for electronic components to be completed.'

This inevitably means that Pat's job is very much a management role these days. The thought of that had worried him, to the point where he initially turned the job down. He's glad he changed his mind.

You could buy three F3000 cars for the cost of our wind tunnel model

---

'I really enjoyed hands-on involvement, but having been through so many areas of engineering, I thought, well, perhaps it was time for a change. I also got a lot of confidence from the fact that a lot of people within Benetton – my peers, really – said I ought to have a go at it, because I would do it well.

'I thought "well, if they're prepared to say that, I'd better give it a go." But it is much more difficult than pure engineering. In engineering there is 90 per cent of the time a mathematical solution to the problem. Management is a juggling act, but it is a lot of fun and one gets a huge amount of satisfaction when you get it right.

'To generate a working environment where people are happy, and operate it cost-effectively, is very enjoyable.'

The Benetton engineering group includes 72 people, 23 of whom are basically designing parts on CAD (computer-aided design) stations in the design office. 'But what is much more relevant is the application of CAE (computer-aided engineering),' explains Symonds. 'It is a lot more now about how you use your mathematical tools to help you with your engineering.

'More modern developments are things like computational fluid dynamics, which enable you to look at initial aerodynamic designs before you even put them into the wind tunnel, improvements in the way you can analyse composite structures, even tools which help you design.

'It is also the integration now into complete factory manufacturing systems; what we are trying to do is to have one company-wide computer system which everyone can use. So from the minute a part is actually conceived, let alone designed, right through to the point where the accountant has to pay for it and the guy in stores has to find it, the whole process is on one system.

'Computers are quite remarkable these days. CAD has enabled us to improve the quality of what we design in almost every way.'

The design and development of every future Benetton F1 machine will be helped enormously by the introduction of a full-sized wind tunnel. 'What

Elegantly laid out foyer at the Benetton F1 base, complete with show car and plenty of trophies to commemorate the team's successes. (Benetton)

'I can't come to England, I've got a GT race!

Alexander Wurz won the BMX World Championship at the age of 12 and feels that the lessons he learned then, riding a competition bicycle, were absolutely crucial in his climb to the upper reaches of F1 competition.

'It was such close racing,' he remembers. 'At the start, like in F1, you had to give everything you had in your muscles, your brain and your body. Even in grand prix racing, if you have got 750bhp, you must always push like hell and that was the same in BMX racing.'

The son of rallycross ace Franz Wurz, Alexander pursued a path through karting and into single seaters where he won the German, Austrian and International Formula Ford Championships in 1992, and the 1993 Austrian F3 title. It was at this time that he started the habit of wearing one blue and one red driving boot. He'd had to borrow a spare boot from a team-mate at one FF race which he promptly went out and won. As a result, he kept what he came to regard as a lucky habit.

Wurz was runner-up in the German F3 Championship in 1994 and two years later moved into the International Touring Car Championship with Opel. During that season he raced against his current Benetton team-mate Fisichella, who was driving an Alfa Romeo, and that, coupled with his 1996 victory with Porsche as the youngest driver ever to win the Le Mans 24

Hour Race, helped him clinch the Benetton test drive in 1997.

'I always knew I wanted to be a racing driver,' he recalls. 'I realised in BMX that if I didn't give 100 per cent all the time, I would never realise my potential. In any professional sport, if you don't try all the time, then you won't cross the line first. It's the same in private life, professional life, whatever.

'I still have the record in my school for swimming over 50-metres, but in class I was very lazy. I was always interested in physics, but not mathematics and I struggled hardest with my English. I went to New Zealand to race Formula Ford not understanding a single word, but came back with a pretty good grasp of it all.'

Wurz admits that his father helped him enormously when it came to financing his kart racing and his first Formula Ford season. He clearly appreciates his father's efforts, but confesses that he did not really learn much from him in terms of car control techniques.

By 1997, Wurz was dovetailing his Benetton testing work with membership of the Mercedes international GT driver squad. Then Gerhard Berger began to suffer from increasingly serious sinus problems and the word came from Benetton that Alex might have to fly to Canada.

'There is a funny story attaching to this,' he grins. 'Firstly the Benetton secretary called me and said, "you must come to England." So I replied, "no, I'm going to a GT race."

'Then the team manager called me. "You should come to England today," he said. I replied, "no, I'm leaving now for the airport. I've got a GT race this weekend!" I still didn't get the message!

'Then Flavio Briatore rang me and said, "right, you'd better come to England now." So I went over, still with all my Mercedes GT kit with me. Flavio said, "it may be that you will race in Canada. We've organised you a flight over in Concorde. If you don't race, we've organised you a flight back in time for first practice for the GT race." So I didn't even know when I was on the plane over to New York whether I would be racing or not.'

Wurz – who in just his first full F1 season was being linked to Ferrari – admits that he is not in the slightest bit concerned about any inexperience which he and Fisichella bring to the job. 'This has not been a problem. Even last year (1997) all the decisions I made as far as set-up work was concerned was always agreed 100 per cent by the race drivers (Alesi and Berger) and I think this is one of the reasons why I was offered a permanent drive this year despite the fact that I had only done three races last year.'

Away from the circuits, as well as following a strict training regime, Alex enjoys skiing, snowboarding, squash and mountain biking. Engaged to Karin, he lives in Monaco.

'I am not contracted with Benetton to just go on slow Sunday afternoon drives,' he says firmly. 'I have to go for it. Last year, the team finished third in the Constructors' Championship, so if Giancarlo and I can achieve that again this year, it would be great.'

Alexander Wurz has his lucky charms in the footwear department! (Formula One Pictures)

Top *One of the Whiteways conference rooms.* (Benetton)

Above *Overall effect within the factory is light and spacious, providing pleasant working conditions for personnel.* (Benetton)

Right *Benetton race cars are worked on by engineers within individually allotted bays in the race shop.* (Benetton)

we decided was that we would build a full-sized wind tunnel that we could put a completed car into, but in fact we would continue doing our testing at 50 per cent scale.

'This scale is easy to get realism out of – easy being a relative term – but the sheer cost of our wind tunnel models would horrify people! You could probably buy three Formula 3000 cars for the cost of our wind tunnel model (over £250,000) and it has to be carefully designed. You must remember that the loads on a 50 per cent model running at 60-metres per second are very high, so it must be structurally intact. But it would not be economic to build a full-scale wind tunnel model.

'For example, to build a new rear wing for the real car could be as much as eight weeks' work. In the wind tunnel you need to cut that down because you need to evaluate many different designs, and the only way of cutting it down is to employ much simpler manufacturing techniques.'

Symonds says that it is quite difficult to pinpoint how many complete cars the team builds during the course of a racing season. 'Most seasons we build seven monocoques, which amounts to basically four on the race team, two on the test team and one to take account of write-offs or experimental work.

'There will always be at least ten sets of suspension around, but this will

Benetton Technical Director Pat Symonds explains to author Alan Henry just how it is. (Formula One Pictures)

change endlessly during the course of the year. By mid-way through 1998 we were on our Mark 5 suspension and Mark 3 rear suspension.

'By the time we complete our new car for the season, hopefully before the previous Christmas, we will have produced about 4,500 drawings and manufactured about 10,000 components. By the time the following season has finished we could get as high as 11,000 drawings before we complete the development of the car.

'As for finalising the design of the following year's car, there are two different philosophies. You can leave it late, as McLaren did in 1998, which worked pretty well for them. But we like to have the new car ready to have a preliminary shakedown run prior to Christmas which gives you the slight buffer of the holiday period to react to any problems.

'We have a nominal date of 15 December to run the first of next year's cars. That means aerodynamic testing from the start of the previous May, and the really detailed design work – bearing in mind lead-in times for manufacturing new components – gets underway by the beginning of July.

'By the time you are in the middle of August the whole design office is really working flat out on next year's car. We have to allow some time for problem solving, and some capacity for development of the existing car.'

On a personal level, Symonds, who is married with five children, found the pressure involved in presiding over the design process of the new Benetton B198 meant that there was just no time for him to take a holiday over the winter. He doesn't complain, though, relishing the challenges that each day brings. He says, quite simply, 'this is the best job of my life'.

Pressure draws the best from people and bonds you as a team

David Richards – himself married with three children – admits that working unsocial hours, and the effect this has on families, is hard on all team members. That is one of the costs of F1. 'I'm very conscious of it. But I've never demanded anything of anybody else that I wouldn't demand more of myself. I know the toll it takes on my own family life, the pressures and the tolerance that Karen (his wife) has had all these years she's been with me. But on the other hand, I do feel that teams work best under a certain element of pressure. I don't mean excessive pressure, but pressure draws the best out of people and draws you together as a team. I also think small, compact teams are more efficient than larger groups.'

Chapter 6

Managing
for change

The 1997 Luxembourg Grand Prix was the last at which Flavio Briatore would preside over the Benetton team. After months of detailed negotiations the position of Chief Executive was taken by David Richards, Chairman and majority shareholder of Prodrive, the highly respected Banbury-based motorsport consultancy which had consistently grabbed the international rally headlines in recent years thanks to the exploits of its Subarus driven by Carlos Sainz and Colin McRae.

Having been asked by British American Tobacco whether Prodrive might consider establishing its own F1 team when the giant tobacco conglomerate began to assess plans for a grand prix involvement, Richards bravely declined.

Although his BAT credentials were well established via the 555 brand sponsorship of his rally team, Richards felt that his organisation did not have the infrastructure in place to take on

such a task. As an alternative, he strongly recommended BAT to approach Benetton.

'Our proposal was rejected,' he explained, 'but during those discussions, we found a certain synergy between our two organisations, so the Benetton family asked me to come aboard anyway.'

At Nurburgring, on his first appearance in Benetton team gear, Richards admitted that his initial task in F1 would be to watch and learn. 'I have a total mandate to control the business,' he said, 'but I will draw a line between the commercial and technical sides and leave the engineers to get on and do their jobs. I am not under-estimating the task ahead of me. It will be a big challenge.'

As for Briatore's future, the picture

Looking to the future? Not even half way through his first full season in F1 Alexander Wurz was being linked with Ferrari. (Formula One Pictures)

remained unclear. There was speculation at the Nurburgring that he might go into business with Bernie Ecclestone, but the FIA Vice President put out a press release saying that he never had any business dealings with Flavio, or any of his companies, 'other than through the Benetton team'. Briatore's only comment on his departure from F1 was that he planned to take a three month break. Yet Benetton had of course not heard the last of 'Flav'.

For the meantime, Richards took a balanced view of his new job. To him, surmounting potential problems was a question of breaking them up into manageable, bite-sized chunks, and formulating a long-term strategy. And then sticking to it.

'Yes, I am a great subscriber to the long game theory,' he cheerfully admitted. 'I think I have been very fortuitous in arriving at Benetton now, because I firmly believe that I am in the right place at the right time. The ingredients for success are all here – talent, enthusiasm, team spirit, all waiting to be motivated. I hope I can now paint the picture which enables everybody here to realise their potential.'

Benetton, of course, had traditionally been portrayed as Flavio Briatore's team. Sure, the Benetton family owned it, but Briatore's free-wheeling, extrovert style meant that one man's identity was stamped firmly on the whole operation. He was the gravelly-voiced chain smoker who courted the media and made the pages of the fashionable glossy magazines. Yet we never really quite knew who he was. Where did he spring from? What was his background?

Richards could hardly have been more different. He started out aiming to be an RAF pilot and won a university scholarship, only to miss the requisite A-level grades. His father

Supportive when times get hard. The 1998 San Marino Grand Prix was unlucky for the Benetton drivers. Fisichella and Wurz (seen here) both failed to finish. (Formula One Pictures)

suggested he try accountancy as a business baseline, after which he could perhaps attack something else. It seems to have been sound advice.

'It taught me a discipline which has served me well in business and certainly gave me a direction,' he admits. What followed prior to the Benetton job is now a matter of history – top rally co-driver, then founder of Prodrive.

So how was David Richards going to change Benetton and revive their fortunes? 'The Benetton board gave me a mandate and full support for a three year plan for the team,' he explains. 'My ideas totally concurred with them and we are clear about what we have to do.

'I want Benetton to have a culture and personality of its own. The team has grappled with the same problems

Rallying call for new brand identity

David Richards is one of those rare individuals who has managed to channel what began as a raw, passionate enthusiasm for motorsport into a prosperous full-time career. He has achieved this by tempering that underlying interest with a keen business sense.

In the 1970s he made his name as a rally co-driver, working with the factory teams of Leyland, Nissan, Opel and Ford over a period of six years, and won the 1981 World Rally Championship as Ari Vatanen's partner in a Rothmans-backed Ford Escort. Yet Richards could see that this chapter of his professional life had obvious limitations; there was only so far he could go in the co-driving role and only so long he could sustain a competitive presence. In a nutshell, it wasn't something he needed to be doing when he was 50.

His company David Richards Autosport Limited, a motorsport consultancy, required all his energy when he retired from competition at the end of 1981. In 1984 he formed his own rally team, and two years later restructured the business to launch Prodrive, which has gone from strength to strength as a multi-functional motorsport consultancy. Prodrive enjoyed successful racing and rallying relationships with manufacturers including Porsche, BMW, Austin Rover, Alfa Romeo, Subaru, and Honda.

The rallying partnership with Subaru delivered one World Champion drivers' title with Colin McRae, and three successive manufacturers' crowns in 1995, 1996 and 1997. Prodrive today not only runs the World Rally Championship Subarus, but in 1998 fielded the works Hondas in the British Touring Car Championship. Next year (1999) Prodrive is set to run the factory Ford Mondeos in this same series and, it is whispered, may well eventually take over the operation of Ford's World Championship rally programme as well.

In 1987, Prodrive's first year of trading, it turned over £1.7 million. That had expanded to £47 million by 1997 which made Richards, still only in his mid-40s, an extremely rich man.

He claims that his accountancy background has helped enormously in shaping his essentially pragmatic view of the motorsport team management role. 'There are times when you have to accept second best, because you know that unless you do that this year, there will not be a business left next year. There are so many people I see who disregard that.

'Having said that, only relatively recently did we sit down and appraise in detail the way in which the Prodrive business had developed. In the early days, I did everything on gut reaction, a slightly opportunistic approach which meant we would tackle anything on a short-term approach if it looked as though it would be profitable.

'That's how we started touring car racing; we had a pile of bits in the corner of the workshop when Frank Sytner walked in one day and suddenly we were building him a BMW 3-series racer. Then about five years ago I began to realise that we could not continue like this any longer and that we needed to rationalise.'

When Richards arrived at Benetton one

of the first things he produced was a mission statement outlining his basic vision of how the team would develop over the next few years.

'I think many teams have an identity which comes from circumstance,' he explains. 'My aim is to create a company which has an identity that is clearly differentiated from the rest, and we need to do that in a very strategic way.

'Today, I believe that Ferrari is the only team which, so far, has a clear "stand alone" identity. Most other teams are a sub-set of Formula 1. They might be identified by enthusiasts, but they certainly do not stand out in their own right to the man in the street. They are too dependent on transient elements such as drivers and sponsors. It is not like the "good old days" where you have the Mercedes Silver Arrows, Lotus and Ferrari and those issues need to be re-captured.'

Richards is determined that Benetton will develop a brand identity which clearly marks the team out as different from the opposition. 'That is the only way forward. I think some teams – perhaps like McLaren and Williams – have been driven by a passion for F1 in the narrowest sense of the word.

'It's been clearly successful, of course, so there is no way it can be condemned. It has worked for its time, but I think the new way for the future is to be far broader with your approach and fully understand all the assets you have at your disposal.

'The simplistic thought of an F1 team is that we have X-square feet of space on our motor car and the facility to host people in the Paddock Club. That is simplistic in the extreme. What we have to do is broaden the opportunity out to the widest possible audience, the widest possible number of consumers, thereby stabilising the income stream of the company so it is not reliant on one major investor – such as a cigarette company – and give a firmer basis for the business in the long term.'

Richards plans to translate the rallying success and consistency he achieved with Asian and European partners into F1 glory for Benetton. He aims to establish the team as 'an Anglo-Italian combination, of British engineering and organisation with Latin flair'.

David Richards, thoughts about future business strategies are never far from his mind. (Formula One Pictures)

117

faced by every top F1 entrant over the past ten years, growing from 78 personnel in 1988 to just 300 on January 1st. Once you get over about 200 people you have to stop running it like a small business and have a much more structured approach. We experienced this at Prodrive where, I admit, we went through real problems.

'I think that, from now on, the personality cult has to be avoided at Benetton. There was a perception from the outside that it was dominated by one individual.

'But simply to say that the team had lost its direction is too simple a way of presenting it. Clearly losing a driver of Michael Schumacher's calibre would make an impact on any team. I think in such circumstances there is a danger that the team lets such a loss get it down. But I think the quality of the people here at Enstone is of a very high order and we have to make it known they are appreciated and contributing to the overall effort.'

Richards expressed confidence that Technical Director Pat Symonds and Chief Designer Nick Wirth now understand the problems which made the performance of the B197 chassis so inconsistent. 'That certainly blighted the year,' he conceded, 'but now we are confident about our technical direction.

'Some people expect results at the flick of a light switch, but F1 just isn't

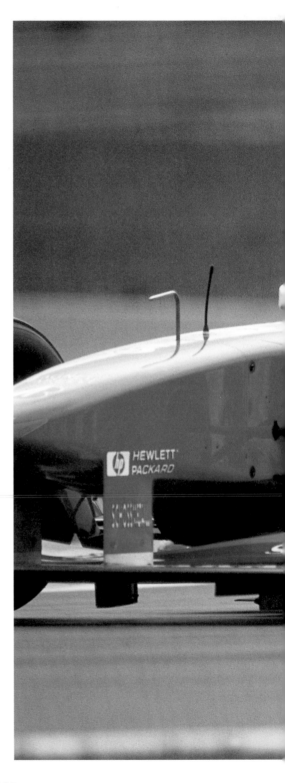

Giancarlo Fisichella on his way to a splendid second place behind Michael Schumacher's Ferrari in the 1998 Canadian Grand Prix. (Formula One Pictures)

like that. I've been a great observer of what Jean Todt has been doing at Ferrari over the past few years. Working away quietly, getting all the elements together and methodically getting results. That is what we now have to do at Benetton.'

Managing the euphoria of success is very difficult

Richards, while undoubtedly a tough task master when the situation demands it, presents a humane approach that is not obvious at the top of every F1 team. Indeed he is regarded by some as almost a father figure to his two young drivers. 'I think the age differential is big enough for me to offer that sort of support, and I guess I've worked with enough drivers over the years for people to see that my opinion has some validity.

'I think if I have one asset that I feel comfortable with, it is my ability to get the best out of people.

'There are never cut-and-dried reasons for people not going so well. Fisichella at the start of the 1998 season wasn't on the form that he should have been. Wurz went through a more difficult period mid-season. But they can draw themselves out of this, and I think the responsibility for this rests largely with the management team around them. If people have that talent then it is our responsibility to give them the best opportunity to express it.'

Some people thought that Richards might have been over-stretched trying to run both Benetton and Prodrive. In fact, the only problem arose when his switch to the F1 team was brought forward two months – 'originally, it was scheduled for the beginning of December 1997'.

Yet his decision to relinquish day-to-day control of Prodrive was by then already well underway. 'I suppose I will still spend around 10 per cent of my time on Prodrive matters,' he says. 'Board meetings and debating strategic issues, things like that.'

At Benetton his main priority is to keep the team on a steady track, with no spectacular or immediate changes. That doesn't just mean coaxing, cajoling and inspiring the workforce into following his lead, but also educating them to understand his personal business credo.

'Outsiders, including some people in the media, consider Formula 1 and other leading forms of motorsport as purely technical exercises. But in this business it is people that win. Lose sight of that, and you are lost.

'Managing the euphoria of success – which Benetton has experienced in the past – is very difficult and does not automatically happen. So, clearly, I think Benetton has been through a very tricky period over the past couple of years, but the reality is that the people who did all the groundwork for the Michael Schumacher World Championship years are still all here.

'However, when I arrived here, one of the things which surprised me was that the relationship between the factory here at Enstone and Benetton

Alexander Wurz at the 1998 French Grand Prix where he finished fifth. (Formula One Pictures)

Left *Pit garages are functional places but you'd think they could manage a chair.* (Formula One Pictures)

Right *Rocco Benetton, bridging the gap.* (Benetton Formula)

in Italy was very remote. So Luciano Benetton's youngest son Rocco has come over to work with me on this and we are trying to bridge the gap more effectively.'

Differences in approach between rallying and F1? 'The thing I see about the F1 side is that many of the engineers at a younger age get pocketed into a particular speciality, yet the best designers and engineers are the ones with the wider overview and the more general grasp of things.

'I think rallying, of necessity, spawns that because it is of a more general nature. Having said that, F1 and rallying are heading down the same route, and I've actually changed some of the strategy in our rally team to achieve that.

'Traditionally, rally engineering has been a far bigger compromise, because you are trying to cater for so many more different situations, and the driver is a more significant factor. Personally I believe this is going to move the other way over the next few years, and I think we will be the first team to address the way in which things are going to develop next. You are going to have to spend much more money on the cars, focus a lot more detailed attention on the set-up of the cars for varying conditions, and what I'm seeing here in F1 can be translated into that environment.'

Chapter 7

The commercial edge

Benetton's sponsorship portfolio includes a cross-section of major international corporations which are backed up by a wide range of specialist team suppliers. These are organisations that are not only all fascinated by the alluring image offered by the FIA Formula 1 World Championship, but can prove beyond doubt that grand prix motor racing has a global marketing reach which is matched by few, if any, rival professional sports.

The key title sponsor on the Benetton B198s is Japan Tobacco's Mild Seven cigarette brand, the world's second largest-selling cigarette, while United Colors of Benetton and Playlife – the multi-national sports equipment manufacturing group which included such brands as Nordica, Prince, Kastle and Roller-blade – are, of course, closely associated with the Benetton family.

Other major sponsors include Federal Express, Agip, Korean Air, Akai, Bridgestone, Hewlett Packard, D2 Privat (Telecom), PI. SA Ceramica, Rauch, Minichamps and OMB (household refuse disposal).

As an example of the benefits of F1 sponsorship, Federal Express offers a classic case. 'F1 racing epitomises precision teamwork in an incredibly high pressure environment,' says John Cooper, Vice President of Marketing and Customer Services at Federal Express Canada Ltd.

'Our employees face similar challenges every day, so the Benetton F1 sponsorship was a natural fit. To our customers, Fedex represents speed, reliability and technology. In Benetton's F1 team we have a relationship with another global enterprise that shares similar values.'

In addition, there is the benefit of getting FedEx closer to its customers by using the association with Benetton as a promotional tool. When FedEx opened a new £2 million facility in Birmingham, its close ties with the team was demonstrated by the fact that

Benetton Chief Designer Nick Wirth was guest of honour at the ceremony.

'We were pleased to welcome three winners of recent FedEx contests to the 1998 British Grand Prix,' said Monte Face, FedEx's Managing Director of Operations for the UK and Ireland. 'We also hosted the FedEx Junior Test Day which was an invitation to customers and their children to see Benetton's factory and the pit area at Silverstone during a test session where they were thrilled to have a photo session with Alexander Wurz.'

Other partnerships, such as that with Hewlett Packard, have a more direct bearing on Benetton's day-to-day F1 involvement. The team uses HP workstations for many of its design processes and HP products are also used to assist the engineers in the task of analysing the huge amount of telemetry data which is received from the cars themselves.

As far as meshing the differing sponsorship requirements is concerned, David Richards and his colleagues have been quietly successful in making sure that the team is not aligned with the avante garde, not to say tasteless, shock tactics of some of the recent Benetton corporate advertising campaigns.

However, there are also more important longer-term sponsorship issues which require urgent attention. Recent EEC legislation means that the clock is now ticking towards the banning of F1 cigarette sponsorship in Europe. So where does Richards see the Benetton F1 operation positioned by the end of that period?

'I think it is important to establish

Benetton in business. An artistic-looking Berger slams round Parabolica in the 1986 Italian GP during the team's first full season under the clothing company's name. (Formula One Pictures)

what sort of brand identity we choose for ourselves,' he said. 'Who we are, what we stand for and what the visual impact we offer should be. We should have established that clearly by the end of 1998, but there will be a lot of debate in the meantime to define that.

'I have explained that all in conceptual terms to the Benetton family, and to the workforce at Enstone, but we need to distil that down into key elements and then to start changing things from within. We have to establish the basic cultural values of the business, saying that this is the way we will behave, this will be the way we respond to our clients, and towards our staff. Once that is established within the company, we will continue to project that image to the outside world.

'It is a bit like joining a club of like-minded people. Likewise for sponsors, it is possible that, once we have established our brand identity, some of them might feel we are inappropriate for their needs. I think that is unlikely, as it happens, but we need to get away from the mentality that the best sponsor is simply the one with the biggest suitcase full of money.

'There are so many aspects of the team to consider. Firstly, the winning. The team must be successful, that is one key dimension. Secondly, the team must be profitable. You cannot continue to invest in this business without actually making money.

Making the most of your photo opportunities. The Benetton squad line up to be snapped with supermodel Eva Herzegova in Spain, 1995. (Formula One Pictures)

Thirdly, the team must maintain its own brand image and identity. That is the element which is too easy to miss.'

Richards feels that if a team totally concentrates on performance, the moment that performance slumps, you are of little value. 'You have nothing else to offer. But if you are a Ferrari, if you are not successful, you are still creating value. And if you do the two together, you become a super-team.'

Benetton has a very solid team of people working on the technical side, but too much of the recent profits have perhaps been taken out of the business rather than re-invested into creating a fresh image.

Richards believes he has no great difficulty in getting his mind around the challenge involved, feeling that the differences between handling a top F1 team and a World Rally Championship contender is really very subtle.

'Aside from the obvious fact that one goes round and round in circles and the other goes up and down mountains, F1 and rallying appeal to and attract very different audiences. So the assets and the profile of rallying offer a very distinct identity which marks it out from F1. The structures of the team are different, but there I think there are sufficient parallels which enabled me to draw on experiences in the past, giving me an insight on how to handle the new challenges.

'I have deliberately taken a low profile, both in the factory and in the

F1 paddock, because I feel I need to understand more of the issues involved in grand prix racing before laying down any personal markers.'

As far as Giancarlo Fisichella and Alexander Wurz are concerned, Richards believes that their arrival on the Benetton scene has been an absolute delight for team morale, as well as being a very positive attraction for existing and future sponsors.

'We have long contracts with them

What the sponsors like to see. Victory in the 1995 Pacific GP at Japan's Aida circuit, and Michael puts his second World Championship beyond any challenge. (Formula One Pictures)

both and they are a very impressive young pairing,' he says. 'I met them for the first time at the end of last year and was struck by the fact that they are very different characters.

'Alexander is a very single-minded, thoughtful and intense person and perhaps reflects his upbringing with a slightly Germanic approach to things. A more polite, delightful, boy-next-door type of character you couldn't wish to meet. He is a really thoughtful person and a great team player, as indeed is Giancarlo. And if there is one single factor which has changed the morale in this organisation, it is not the arrival of me, but the arrival of those two drivers.

'Giancarlo, by contrast, is slightly more flamboyant, more Italian, a complete natural talent. Not somebody to be under-estimated. He and Alex both complement each other and help each other a great deal. But they

New partnership. David Richards with Luciano Benetton in 1997 just before he took up the role of Benetton F1 Chief Executive. (Formula One Pictures)

Richards with Bernie Ecclestone, the FIA Vice President Public Affairs and the most powerful man in Formula 1. (Formula One Pictures)

Appreciated asset

The Benetton Group – whose Sportsystem brands complement the traditional casual collections for men, women and children – is now one of the biggest textile and clothing groups in the world, with a total turnover of 4,200 billion lire. It says the breakthroughs achieved in the F1 team's own laboratories are turned to good use in the development and production of sports equipment and performance wear.

'Our F1 commitment obviously costs us money,' says Luciano Benetton, co-founder of the company which gave a new meaning to the ·words publicity vehicle. 'But we have also gained a lot of prestige, and our overall image has certainly benefited.

'At the beginning of our involvement we weren't quite up to scratch, but then we started to win races and Championships. We started to be appreciated for what we achieved, and we are very proud of that.

'From a showbusiness point of view it would be great if there was a driver from each of the countries which host a grand prix. But our aim is to nurture talent, irrespective of nationality. It is a double bonus with someone like Fisichella, [an Italian driving for an Italian team] who has also got what it takes to become a World Champion.'

The Benetton Group says its 'passion for life and sport' is also demonstrated through its basketball and rugby teams, both at the top of their championship leagues in 1997, and volleyball.

Happy families. Celebrating their second World Championship, the jubilant Benetton squad pose en masse. (Formula One Pictures)

are so different. Giancarlo would be out until the small hours in a disco, whereas Alex might rather have a quiet night in with a book. But the enthusiasm and commitment they both bring is enormous. They bring 100 per cent effort bar nothing to the whole equation.'

Part of the drivers' work involves talking with sponsors at grand prix weekends, attending functions, and generally being pleasant to the nice people who help fund their team. 'The drivers complain a lot about that,' says Richards, 'but the reality is that, without that sort of financial investment, they wouldn't earn anything like what they are getting today.

'We tend to keep things to a minimum, but when I've heard people complaining in the past, I've consulted my diary and found that most drivers are occupied for less than half the days that their engineering staff put in, and certainly less than the average person in the street. For example I think Alain Prost is finding that being a team owner is taking a lot more out of him than winning those four World Championships ever did as a driver!'

Chapter

The
race weekend

The operation of the Benetton F1 team over race weekends – and indeed, the administration of the factory apart from design and financial matters – is the responsibility of 42-year-old Joan Villadelprat whose official title is Formula Operations Director/Team Manager.

A cheerful, enthusiastic Spaniard, Joan – pronounced Joanne – is one of the most seasoned operators in the F1 business. He started his career as a mechanic in Spanish national racing formulae in 1972 and eventually graduated to F1 with McLaren in 1979 where he stayed until 1986.

From 1987 to 1989 he was chief mechanic on the Ferrari F1 team, only leaving to accept the post of team manager at Tyrrell. Then he moved to Benetton where he spent the first three years as Operations Manager, taking over his present role in 1993 just as Michael Schumacher was getting into his stride for the golden years of the team's achievement so far.

Joan explains that the team's preparation for any European race begins around the previous weekend when all three cars designated for use at a particular event are given a routine shakedown trial. 'Normally we do the shakedown on the previous Friday afternoon or Saturday morning at Silverstone or the Santa Pod drag strip. This is just to enable us to go up and down through the gears, make sure all the systems work and that's it.

'After that's been done, the trucks go back to the factory. Basically the other transporters have already been loaded and only a few additional extras need to be readied before the transporters depart on the Saturday evening or the Sunday you leave, depending on whether it takes two days or three days to get to the race concerned.'

The Benetton race team has three Renault transporters. One articulated truck takes up to four cars plus the general office. Then there is an articulated support truck which contains the

Spotless, neatly-lined transporters and well-regimented tyres is the order of the day from Bernie. Strict professionalism is expected at all times. (Formula One Pictures)

Race morning, and the Benetton B198 race cars wait on their stands for the wheels to be fitted and the action to begin. (Nick Henry)

workshop area plus spares, and another vehicle with a rigid chassis which carries all the pit equipment and material to fit out the garage. Each has two drivers in order to conform with the EEC tachograph regulations.

In a big team you can send a plane home to fetch parts

'The transporters normally arrive at the circuit on Tuesday night or Wednesday morning at the latest, because it takes quite a long time to set up the garage. Then we send some of the electronics people and mechanics on Wednesday, followed by the rest of the crew who arrive on Thursday.

'In total, including the people from marketing and the management, we are about 45 people at each race, most of whom travel on the special F1 charter flights.' These are usually organised by Travel Places, the Arundel-based specialist travel agency headed by Bob Warren who has been in this line of business for well over 20 years and whose staff are well tuned to the needs of the F1 fraternity.

At all the races, Joan tries to ensure that the mechanics stay in hotels as close to the track as possible, in case they need to work very late dealing with some unexpected emergency. 'Every year this tends to get more difficult, but because we have long established relationships with some hotels, what we often do is to book for the following year as soon as we finish the current grand prix – and sometimes for the next two years.'

With free practice on Fridays not starting until 11.00am, the mechanics arrive at the circuit at about 8.00am and have their breakfast at the team's motorhome before starting work. On Saturday, when the practice schedule starts at 9.00am, the Benetton crew arrives between 6.30 and 6.45am and the same applies on race day.

It is Villadeprat's plan that the team should always finish any preparation work required on the cars in the evenings; nothing is left unfinished for the following morning. 'The cars are completely ready before we go to bed, however long it takes,' he grins. 'The cars are left on the stands, off the ground, so in theory all you have to do the following morning is to put in the fuel and polish the paintwork.

'Usually the schedule is not too bad, because the cars are generally going well, we have a lot of spares available and we are backed up with a big factory with considerable resources. We come to the races with the engines and gearboxes all really kitted up for fitting into the cars, so it's not as bad as it used to be.

'If everything goes smoothly the boys probably get to bed between 11.00pm and midnight, although obviously sometimes it's necessary to work all night if you have a shunt or a major accident. We tend to manage this even on Saturday and that has progressively improved over the years.

'Obviously at the start of the season it is a little more delicate because the team is tending to get to know the car,

After the warm-up, final preparation should only involve a few loving touches and some gentle polishing! (Nick Henry)

and you are often short of spares, but by the middle of the year we are usually well under control. When you are in a big team, you always have the resources – we even have the ability in Europe, if necessary, to send a plane back home to get some bits and bring them out. It's different when you are in a small team; I remember it was a bit more delicate!'

These drivers are brilliant to work with – keen, fast, and quick to learn

---

Joan clearly subscribes to the view that an army marches on its stomach. Like other modern F1 teams, Benetton sees that its workforce is properly fed and watered at all times. 'Every day they have a proper lunch and dinner, sitting down under the awning outside the team motorhome. On race day they will have sandwiches at lunchtime and after the race there is a proper cooked meal, even though many of them will be leaving on the F1 charter flight that evening, usually around 6.00pm on the Sunday.

'We leave behind a group of mechanics and the six truck drivers to pack up the rest of the equipment, although after the warm-up on race morning a lot of the material is already packed up with the intention of allowing the truck to leave by about ten o'clock from the circuit. Budapest and Jerez are about the furthest tracks from base in Europe, and the trucks tend to

get back to Enstone by about Tuesday lunchtime at the latest after the race, although sometimes they can be back on Monday evening from races which are not too far away.'

As the race weekend unfolds, so Benetton's marketing department organises the hosting of its VIP guests in the Paddock Club, most of whom are representatives from the team's many sponsors, investors and suppliers. The number of such guests can vary wildly depending on the race concerned, but at the 1998 British Grand Prix the team entertained approximately 140 on the Friday, 200 on the Saturday, and 260 on race day.

The responsibility for looking after these guests falls on Mary Warren, Sophy Williams, Geraldine Paphouse and Fiona Sprague. The team's Commercial Director David Warren – who started his F1 career in sponsorship liaison, working on the Canon sponsorship programme with the Williams team in the mid-1980s – will liaise with guests and representatives from sponsors' senior management, as well as working closely with David Richards in a bid to maximise any future sponsorship prospects and possibilities.

Throughout the weekend there will also be continuous pressure from the media for interviews with Alexander Wurz, Giancarlo Fisichella and David Richards, so press officers Andrea Ficarelli and Julia Horden have their hands full fielding such inquiries and slotting them into a detailed schedule

Giancarlo Fisichella remains cool and relaxed in the run-up to the race start.
(Nick Henry)

138

It's important to get to know each other well so that the teamwork becomes instinctive. (Formula One Pictures)

Left *Alexander Wurz is refuelled on his way to fourth place in the 1998 Spanish Grand Prix.* (Formula One Pictures)

which starts on the Thursday prior to the race.

However, by race morning the drivers tend to be shielded from such requests as they complete the warm-up, confer with the engineers over any changes necessary to the cars prior to the start of the race, and then try to get an hour or so of relaxation in the team's motorhome before going to the grid.

Both Fisichella and Wurz are remarkably laid-back in the run-up to the race, their youthful enthusiasm tempered by considerable inner confidence. There are no untoward attacks of nerves [or the last-minute gallop to the gents required by certain top drivers] as the time comes for them to be strapped into the cockpit.

Accurately predicting the weather on race day is an exercise which puts great demands on a contemporary F1 team. At Silverstone in 1998 there was clearly a chance of rain, but David Richards wanted to have more precise information at his disposal and drew on his extensive rally expertise by sending up his helicopter with David Warren to accompany the pilot.

They flew into the wind and, despite reports from local airfields that the impending rain showers would miss Silverstone, correctly reported back that a downpour was indeed coming and enabled the team to make precisely the correct tyre choice which certainly helped Alexander and

Giancarlo to climb through the pack to finish an eventual fourth and fifth.

It is perhaps inevitable with two young drivers that the occasional accident will blunt their progress. Wurz was fortunate to emerge unscathed from a first corner accident in the 1998

Youthful single-mindedness. During his alarming-looking first corner shunt in the 1998 Canadian Grand Prix, Wurz's first thought was to call the pits and ask if he could use the spare car. (ICN UK Bureau)

Canadian Grand Prix at Montreal where he barrel-rolled over and over into the gravel trap after colliding with Jean Alesi's Sauber. Yet even as he was somersaulting his main priority was to ask over the radio whether he could have the spare car for the restart. He

did – and finished fourth!

Joan regards the team's two youngsters as 'just brilliant'. He says, 'I've been about 19 years in F1 now, working for a lot of good teams. But these two guys are brilliant to work with, they listen to what you have to say, they are

Rocco Benetton – hugely excited to work in F1

Rocco Benetton is 29 years old, wide-eyed and effusively enthusiastic in his role as Vice President of the Benetton F1 team. Son of the knitwear empire's co-founder Luciano Benetton, he is assistant to Chief Executive David Richards, providing an important new link between the UK-based team and the Benetton group in Italy.

'When Benetton first came into F1 with the Tyrrell team in 1983, our most important consideration was on the marketing side, simply to have a return on our investment by enhancing the group's image,' he explains. 'It was a question of getting that brand known on a wider global basis.

'Today we have achieved that aim and moved further. We now have a winning image and, over the years, what we have gained for the group has been very high. 'Times have changed, of course. The actual United Colors of Benetton mother group and the Benetton Formula branding are now known independently by everybody.'

Rocco's hands-on involvement in the F1 business follows experience in other areas of commerce. After completing his high school education in Italy, he continued with undergraduate engineering studies in the USA where he also learned about Benetton's retailing activities.

'After that I went into the stock market and worked on Wall Street for seven years. I spent time both on the trading floor and on asset management work.

'I think my presence at Enstone emphasises that there was a need for the Benetton group to become directly involved in the F1 team. Not so much as a family member, you understand, because Benetton is now a public company, so I like to think that I am looking after the interests of all those associated with the group, shareholders, family, everybody.

'I have a great deal to learn and have committed 100 per cent of my efforts to the task. I hope before long I will be able to contribute positively. I spend most of my time at Enstone; if I am not there, it is because I am travelling on F1 business.

'I work closely with David Richards. He is responsible for running the team, day-by day, although he is learning as well about F1 as he basically comes from a different business. But we both have to make sure that we satisfy all the needs of the Benetton group, from the communications standpoint, marketing, everything.

'I was born into the United Colors of Benetton Group, so I know how they think and what their needs are, and I have to be able to translate and apply this knowledge to the Benetton F1 business.'

Rocco was a passionate motor racing fan long before his family became involved in F1 sponsorship. 'In Italy, it is a very easy thing to become addicted to. I remember in 1983 going with my father to Ken Tyrrell when the team's sponsorship arrangement was announced. I was 13 years old, but I still remember very well the excitement of going there and meeting with the idols whom we had only previously known on television. And to this day it remains hugely exciting for me to be involved in Formula 1.'

A pit garage marches on its stomach. (Formula One Pictures)

learning quickly and are very fast. It was the most important element of the entire team in 1998.'

Back at the factory Joan and his assistant Mark Owen have their hands well and truly full with the overall administration of the team's day-to-day operations. 'I am also in charge of all the production and operation of the factory as well, apart from the design or finding the money, everything else is on my shoulders.'

Look closely at the 1998 Benetton team and you will see a cohesive, committed and, above all, bubblingly enthusiastic F1 operation which, for all the credit accorded to the drivers, reflects very positively on David Richards's precise yet unfussy management style.

People are very much allowed to get on with their jobs with the minimum of red tape and management bureaucracy. The evidence is that, in such an intense business where everybody is focused on making a success of the whole opera-

tion, this approach works well.

Joan Villadelprat and Pat Symonds both reflect Richards's modus operandi, albeit a step down the management chain. 'I would like to think that our people are happy,' says Joan, 'although there is always a danger when a company gets much bigger that it can become impersonal. It gets very difficult to maintain the family atmosphere.

'But the entire management at Benetton understands that this is very important. My door is open at any time for everybody from a senior engineer to the office cleaner, and Pat is just the same. We try to be very approachable. We take any criticism from anybody, irrespective of their position in the company, as long as it is positive.

'I think that is unique in F1. The workforce is not afraid to talk to us and I think that is responsible for sustaining the positive mood which we have at the moment. Benetton has always been a happy team in my experience, and I would like it to remain that way.'

Appendix 1

Benetton – race results

As the Benetton F1 team metamorphosised from the remains of the Toleman F1 operation, these results include all races from Toleman's debut in the 1981 San Marino GP through to the 1998 Austrian Grand Prix.

Key to abbreviations:

R – retired; N – did not start;
C – non classified; Q – did not qualify;
D – disqualified

TOLEMAN, 1981–85

1981

3 May	SAN MARINO GP, Imola		
	B. Henton	Toleman-Hart TG181	Q
	D. Warwick	Toleman-Hart TG181	Q
17 May	BELGIAN GP, Zolder		
	B. Henton	Toleman-Hart TG181	Q
	D. Warwick	Toleman-Hart TG181	Q
31 May	MONACO GP, Monte Carlo		
	B. Henton	Toleman-Hart TG181	Q
	D. Warwick	Toleman-Hart TG181	Q
21 June	SPANISH GP, Jarama		
	B. Henton	Toleman-Hart TG181	Q
	D. Warwick	Toleman-Hart TG181	Q
5 July	FRENCH GP, Dijon-Prenois		
	B. Henton	Toleman-Hart TG181	Q
	D. Warwick	Toleman-Hart TG181	Q
18 July	BRITISH GP, Silverstone		
	B. Henton	Toleman-Hart TG181	Q
	D. Warwick	Toleman-Hart TG181	Q
2 Aug	GERMAN GP, Hockenheim		
	B. Henton	Toleman-Hart TG181	Q
	D. Warwick	Toleman-Hart TG181	Q
16 Aug	AUSTRIAN GP, Osterreichring		
	B. Henton	Toleman-Hart TG181	Q
	D. Warwick	Toleman-Hart TG181	Q
30 Aug	DUTCH GP, Zandvoort		
	B. Henton	Toleman-Hart TG181	Q
	D. Warwick	Toleman-Hart TG181	Q
13 Sep	ITALIAN GP, Monza		
	B. Henton	Toleman-Hart TG181	10
	D. Warwick	Toleman-Hart TG181	Q
27 Sep	CANADIAN GP, Montreal		
	B. Henton	Toleman-Hart TG191	Q
	D. Warwick	Toleman-Hart TG181	Q
17 Oct	CAESARS PALACE GP, Las Vegas		
	B. Henton	Toleman-Hart TG181	Q
	D. Warwick	Toleman-Hart TG181	R

1982

23 Jan   SOUTH AFRICAN GP, Kyalami
D. Warwick   Toleman-Hart TG181C   R
T. Fabi   Toleman-Hart TG181B   Q
21 Mar   BRAZILIAN GP, Rio de Janeiro
D. Warwick   Toleman-Hart TG181C   Q
T. Fabi   Toleman-Hart TG181B   Q
4 Apr   US GP WEST, Long Beach
D. Warwick   Toleman-Hart GT181C   Q
T. Fabi   Toleman-Hart TG181C   Q
25 Apr SAN MARINO GP, Imola
D. Warwick   Toleman-Hart TG181C   R
T. Fabi   Toleman-Hart TG181C   C
9 May   BELGIAN GP, Zolder
D. Warwick   Toleman-Hart TG181C   R
T. Fabi   Toleman-Hart TG181C   R
23 May   MONACO GP, Monte Carlo
D. Warwick   Toleman-Hart TG181C   Q
T. Fabi   Toleman-Hart TG181C   Q
6 Jun   UNITED STATES GP, Detroit
            Entries withdrawn
13 Jun   CANADIAN GP, Montreal
            Entries withdrawn
3 Jul   DUTCH GP, Zandvoort
D. Warwick   Toleman-Hart TG181C   R
T. Fabi   Toleman-Hart TG181C   Q
18 Jul   BRITISH GP, Brands Hatch
D. Warwick   Toleman-Hart TG181C   R
T. Fabi   Toleman-Hart TG181C   R
25 Jul   FRENCH GP, Paul Ricard
D. Warwick   Toleman-Hart TG181C   15
T. Fabi   Toleman-Hart TG181C   R
8 Aug   GERMAN GP, Hockenheim
D. Warwick   Toleman-Hart TG181C   10
T. Fabi   Toleman-Hart TG181C   R
15 Aug   AUSTRIAN GP, Osterreichring
D. Warwick   Toleman-Hart TG181C   R
T. Fabi   Toleman-Hart TG181C   R
29 Aug   SWISS GP, Dijon-Prenois
D. Warwick   Toleman-Hart TG181C   R
T. Fabi   Toleman-Hart TG181C   R
12 Sep   ITALIAN GP, Monza
D. Warwick   Toleman-Hart TG183   R
T. Fabi   Toleman-Hart TG181C   R

25 Sep   CAESARS PALACE GP, Las Vegas
D. Warwick   Toleman-Hart TG183   R
T. Fabi   Toleman-Hart TG181C   Q

1983

13 Mar   BRAZILIAN GP, Rio de Janeiro
D. Warwick   Toleman-Hart TG183B   8
B. Giacomelli Toleman-Hart TG183B   R
27 Mar   US GP WEST, Long Beach
D. Warwick   Toleman-Hart TG183B   R
B. Giacomelli Toleman-Hart TG183B   R
17 Apr   FRENCH GP, Paul Ricard
D. Warwick   Toleman-Hart TG183B   R
B. Giacomelli Toleman-Hart TG183B   13
1 May   SAN MARINO GP, Imola
D. Warwick   Toleman-Hart TG183B   R
B. Giacomelli Toleman-Hart TG183B   R
15 May   MONACO GP, Monte Carlo
D. Warwick   Toleman-Hat TG183B   R
B. Giacomelli Toleman-Hart TG183B   Q
22 May   BELGIAN GP, Spa Francorchamps
D. Warwick   Toleman-Hart TG183B   7
B. Giacomelli Toleman-Hart TG183B   8
5 June   UNITED STATES GP, Detroit
D. Warwick   Toleman-Hart TG183B   R
B. Giacomelli Toleman-Hart TG183B   9
12 Jun   CANADIAN GP, Montreal
D. Warwick   Toleman-Hart TG183B   R
B. Giacomelli Toleman-Hart TG183B   R
16 Jul   BRITISH GP, Silverstone
D. Warwick   Toleman-Hart TG183B   R
B. Giacomelli Toleman-Hart TG183B   R
7 Aug   GERMAN GP, Hockenheim
D. Wawick   Toleman-Hart TG183B   R
B. Giacomelli Toleman-Hart TG183B   R
14 Aug   AUSTRIAN GP, Osterreichring
D. Warwick   Toleman-Hart TG183B   R
B. Giacomelli Toleman-Hart TG183B   R
28 Aug   DUTCH GP, Zandvoort
D. Warwick   Toleman-Hart TG183B   4
B. Giacomelli Toleman-Hart TG183B   13
11 Sep   ITALIAN GP, Monza
D. Warwick   Toleman-Hart TG183B   6
B. Giacomelli Toleman-Hart TG183B   7

25 Sep   GP OF EUROPE, Brands Hatch
    D. Warwick   Toleman-Hart TG183B   5
    B. Giacomelli Toleman-Hart TG183B   6
15 Oct   SOUTH AFRICAN GP, Kyalami
    D. Warwick   Toleman-Hart TG183B   4
    B. Giacomelli Toleman-Hart TG183B   R

1984

Mar 25   BRAZILIAN GP, Rio de Janeiro
    A. Senna   Toleman-Hart TG183B   R
    J. Cecotto   Toleman-Hart TG183B   R
Apr 7   SOUTH AFRICAN GP, Kyalami
    A. Senna   Toleman-Hart TG183B   6
    J. Cecotto   Toleman-Hart TG183B   R
Apr 29   BELGIAN GP, Zolder
    A. Senna   Toleman-Hart TG183B   6
    J. Cecotto   Toleman-Hart TG183B   R
May 6   SAN MARINO GP, Imola
    A. Senna   Toleman-Hart TG183B   Q
    J. Cecotto   Toleman-Hart TG183B   C
May 20   FRENCH GP, Dijon-Prenois
    A. Senna   Toleman-Hart TG184   R
    J. Cecotto   Toleman-Hart TG184   R
Jun 3   MONACO GP, Monte Carlo
    A. Senna   Toleman-Hart TG184   2
    J. Cecotto   Toleman-Hart TG184   R
Jun 17   CANADIAN GP, Montreal
    A. Senna   Toleman-Hart TG184   7
    J. Ceccotto   Toleman-Hart TG184   9
Jun 24   UNITED STATES GP, Detroit
    A. Senna   Toleman-Hart TG184   R
    J. Ceccotto   Toleman-Hart TG184   R
Jul 8   DALLAS GP, Dallas, Texas
    A. Senna   Toleman-Hart TG184   R
    J. Ceccotto   Toleman-Hart TG184   R
Jul 22   BRITISH GP, Brands Hatch
    A. Senna   Toleman-Hart TG184   3
    J. Ceccotto   Toleman-Hart TG184   N
Aug 5   GERMAN GP, Hockenheim
    A. Senna   Toleman-Hart TG184   R
Aug 19   AUSTRIAN GP, Osterreichring
    A. Senna   Toleman-Hart TG184   R
Aug 26   DUTCH GP, Zandvoort
    A. Senna   Toleman-Hart TG184   R

Sep 9   ITALIAN GP, Monza
    S. Johansson   Toleman-Hart TG184   4
    P-L. Martini   Toleman-Hart TG184   Q
Oct 7   GP OF EUROPE, Nurburgring
    A. Senna   Toleman-Hart TG184   R
    S. Johansson   Toleman-Hart TG184   R
Oct 21   PORTUGUESE GP, Estoril
    A. Senna   Toleman-Hart TG184   3
    S. Johansson   Toleman-Hart TG184   11

1985

Following problems with Pirelli tyre contract, Toleman missed the first three races of the season, joining in only at Monaco by which time Benetton had taken a stake in the team.

19 May   MONACO GP, Monte Carlo
    T. Fabi   Toleman-Hart TG185   R
16 Jun   CANADIAN GP, Montreal
    T. Fabi   Toleman-Hart TG185   R
23 Jun   UNITED STATES GP, Detroit
    T. Fabi   Toleman-Hart TG185   R
7 Jul   FRENCH GP, Paul Ricard
    T. Fabi   Toleman-Hart TG185   14
21 Jul   BRITISH GP, Silverstone
    T. Fabi   Toleman-Hart TG185   R
4 Aug   GERMAN GP, Nurburgring
    T. Fabi   Toleman-Hart TG185   R
18 Aug   AUSTRIAN GP, Osterreichring
    T. Fabi   Toleman-Hart TG185   R
    P. Ghinzani   Toleman-Hart TG185   R
25 Aug   DUTCH GP, Zandvoort
    T. Fabi   Toleman-Hart TG185   R
    P. Ghinzani   Toleman-Hart TG185   R
8 Sep   ITALIAN GP, Monza
    T. Fabi   Toleman-Hart TG185   12
    P. Ghinzani   Toleman-Hart TG185   R
15 Sep   BELGIAN GP, Spa Francorchamps
    T. Fabi   Toleman-Hart TG185   R
    P. Ghinzani   Toleman-Hart TG185   R
6 Oct   GP OF EUROPE, Brands Hatch
    T. Fabi   Toleman-Hart TG185   R
    P. Ghinzani   Toleman-Hart TG185   R

19 Oct   SOUTH AFRICAN GP, Kyalami
   T. Fabi   Toleman-Hart TG185   R
   P. Ghinzani Toleman-Hart TG185   R
3 Nov   AUSTRALIAN GP, Adelaide
   T. Fabi   Toleman-Hart TG185   R
   P. Ghinzani Toleman-Hart TG185   R

BENETTON, 1986 to date

1986

23 Mar   BRAZILIAN GP, Rio de Janeiro
   T. Fabi   Benetton-BMW B186   10
   G. Berger   Benetton-BMW B186   6
13 Apr   SPANISH GP, Jerez
   T. Fabi   Benetton-BMW B186   5
   G. Berger   Benetton-BMW B186   6
27 Apr   SAN MARINO GP, Imola
   T. Fabi   Benetton-BMW B186   R
   G. Berger   Benetton-BMW B186   3
11 May   MONACO GP, Monte Carlo
   T. Fabi   Benetton-BMW B186   R
   G. Berger   Benetton-BMW B186   R
25 May   BELGIAN GP, Spa Francorchamps
   T. Fabi   Benetton-BMW B186   7
   G. Berger   Benetton-BMW B186   10
15 Jun   CANADIAN GP, Montreal
   T. Fabi   Benetton-BMW B186   R
   G. Berger   Benetton-BMW B186   R
22 June   UNITED STATES GP, Detroit
   T. Fabi   Benetton-BMW B186   R
   G. Berger   Benetton-BMW B186   R
6 July   FRENCH GP, Paul Ricard
   T. Fabi   Benetton-BMW B186   R
   G. Berger   Benetton-BMW B186   R
13 July   BRITISH GP, Brands Hatch
   T. Fabi   Benetton-BMW B186   R
   G. Berger   Benetton-BMW B186   R
27 July   GERMAN GP, Hockenheim
   T. Fabi   Benetton-BMW B186   R
   G. Berger   Benetton-BMW B186   10
10 Aug   HUNGARIAN GP, Hungaroring
   T. Fabi   Benetton-BMW B186   R
   G. Berger   Benetton-BMW B186   R

17 Aug   AUSTRIAN GP, Osterreichring
   T. Fabi   Benetton-BMW B186   R
   G. Berger   Benetton-BMW B186   7
7 Sept   ITALIAN GP, Monza
   T. Fabi   Benetton-BMW B186   R
   G. Berger   Benetton-BMW B186   5
Sep 21   PORTUGUESE GP, Estoril
   T. Fabi   Benetton-BMW B186   8
   G. Berger   Benetton-BMW B186   R
Oct 12   MEXICAN GP, Mexico City
   T. Fabi   Benetton-BMW B186   R
   G. Berger   Benetton-BMW B186   1
26 Oct   AUSTRALIAN GP, Adelaide
   T. Fabi   Benetton-BMW B186   10
   G. Berger   Benetton-BMW B186   R

1987

12 Apr   BRAZILIAN GP, Rio de Janeiro
   T. Fabi   Benetton-Ford turbo B187   R
   T. Boutsen Benetton-Ford turbo B187   5
3 May   SAN MARINO GP, Imola
   T. Fabi   Benetton-Ford turbo B187   R
   T. Boutsen Benetton-Ford turbo B187   R
17 May   BELGIAN GP, Spa Francorchamps
   T. Fabi   Benetton-Ford turbo B187   R
   T. Boutsen Benetton-Ford turbo B187   R
31 May   MONACO GP, Monte Carlo
   T. Fabi   Benetton-Ford turbo B187   8
   T. Boutsen Benetton-Ford turbo B187   R
21 Jun   UNITED STATES GP, Detroit
   T. Fabi   Benetton-Ford turbo B187   R
   T. Boutsen Benetton-Ford turbo B187   R
5 July   FRENCH GP, Paul Ricard
   T. Fabi   Benetton-Ford turbo B187   5
   T. Boutsen Benetton-Ford turbo B187   R
12 July   BRITISH GP, Silverstone
   T. Fabi   Benetton-Ford turbo B187   6
   T. Boutsen Benetton-Ford turbo B187   7
26 July   GERMAN GP, Hockenheim
   T. Fabi   Benetton-Ford turbo B187   R
   T. Boutsen Benetton-Ford turbo B187   R
9 Aug   HUNGARIAN GP, Hungaroring
   T. Fabi   Benetton-Ford turbo B187   R
   T. Boutsen Benetton-Ford turbo B187   4

16 Aug   AUSTRIAN GP, Osterreichring
   T. Fabi   Benetton-Ford turbo B187   3
   T. Boutsen   Benetton-Ford turbo B187   4
6 Sept   ITALIAN GP, Monza
   T. Fabi   Benetton-Ford turbo B187   7
   T. Boutsen   Benetton-Ford turbo B187   5
20 Sept   PORTUGUESE GP, Estoril
   T. Fabi   Benetton-Ford turbo B187   4
   T. Boutsen   Benetton-Ford turbo B187   14
27 Sept   SPANISH GP, Jerez
   T. Fabi   Benetton-Ford turbo B187   R
   T. Boutsen   Benetton-Ford turbo B187   16
18 Oct   MEXICAN GP, Mexico City
   T. Fabi   Benetton-Ford turbo B187   5
   T. Boutsen   Benetton-Ford turbo B187   R
1 Nov   JAPANESE GP, Suzuka
   T. Fabi   Benetton-Ford turbo B187   R
   T. Boutsen   Benetton-Ford turbo B187   5
15 Nov   AUSTRALIAN GP, Adelaide
   T. Fabi   Benetton-Ford turbo B187   R
   T. Boutsen   Benetton-Ford turbo B187   3

1988

3 Apr   BRAZILIAN GP, Rio de Janeiro
   A. Nannini   Benetton-Ford DFR B188   R
   T. Boutsen   Benetton-Ford DFR B188   7
1 May   SAN MARINO GP, Imola
   A. Nannini   Benetton-Ford DFR B188   6
   T. Boutsen   Benetton-Ford DFR B188   4
15 May   MONACO GP, Monte Carlo
   A. Nannini   Benetton-Ford DFR B188   R
   T. Boutsen   Benetton-Ford DFR B188   8
29 May   MEXICAN GP, Mexico City
   A. Nannini   Benetton-Ford DFR B188   7
   T. Boutsen   Benetton-Ford DFR B188   8
12 Jun   CANADIAN GP, Montreal
   A. Nannini   Benetton-Ford DFR B188   R
   T. Boutsen   Benetton-Ford DFR B188   3
19 Jun   UNITED STATES GP, Detroit
   A. Nannini   Benetton-Ford DFR B188   R
   T. Boutsen   Benetton-Ford DFR B188   3
3 Jul   FRENCH GP, Paul Ricard
   A. Nannini   Benetton-Ford DFR B188   6
   T. Boutsen   Benetton-Ford DFR B188   R

10 Jul   BRITISH GP, Silverstone
   A. Nannini   Benetton-Ford DFR B188   3
   T. Boutsen   Benetton-Ford DFR B188   R
24 Jul   GERMAN GP, Hockenheim
   A. Nannini   Benetton-Ford DFR B188   18
   T. Boutsen   Benetton-Ford DFR B188   6
7 Aug   HUNGARIAN GP, Hungaroring
   A. Nannini   Benetton-Ford DFR B188   R
   T. Boutsen   Benetton-Ford DFR B188   3
28 Aug   BELGIAN GP, Spa Francorchamps
   A. Nannini   Benetton-Ford DFR B188   D
   T. Boutsen   Benetton-Ford DFR B188   D
11 Sept   ITALIAN GP, Monza
   A. Nannini   Benetton-Ford DFR B188   9
   T. Boutsen   Benetton-Ford DFR B188   6
25 Sep   PORTUGUESE GP, Estoril
   A. Nannini   Benetton-Ford DFR B188   R
   T. Boutsen   Benetton-Ford DFR B188   3
2 Oct   SPANISH GP, Jerez
   A. Nannini   Benetton-Ford DFR B188   3
   T. Boutsen   Benetton-Ford DFR B188   9
30 Oct   JAPANESE GP, Suzuka
   A. Nannini   Benetton-Ford DFR B188   5
   T. Boutsen   Benetton-Ford DFR B188   3
13 Nov   AUSTRALIAN GP, Adelaide
   A. Nannini   Benetton-Ford DFR B188   R
   T. Boutsen   Benetton-Ford DFR B188   5

1989

26 Mar   BRAZILIAN GP, Rio de Janeiro
   A. Nannini   Benetton-Ford DFR B188   6
   J. Herbert   Benetton-Ford DFR B188   4
23 Apr   SAN MARINO GP, Imola
   A. Nannini   Benetton-Ford DFR B188   3
   J. Herbert   Benetton-Ford DFR B188   11
7 May   MONACO GP, Monte Carlo
   A. Nannini   Benetton-Ford DFR B188   8
   J. Herbert   Benetton-Ford DFR B188   14
28 May   MEXICAN GP, Mexico City
   A. Nannini   Benetton-Ford DFR B188   4
   J. Herbert   Benetton-Ford DFR B188   15
4 Jun   UNITED STATES GP, Phoenix
   A. Nannini   Benetton-Ford DFR B188   R
   J. Herbert   Benetton-Ford DFR B188   5

18 Jun   CANADIAN GP, Montreal

A. Nannini   Benetton-Ford DFR B188   D

J. Herbert   Benetton-Ford DFR B188   Q

9 Jul   FRENCH GP, Paul Ricard

A. Nannini   Benetton-Ford V8 B189   R

E. Pirro   Benetton-Ford DFR B188   9

16 Jul   BRITISH GP, Silverstone

A. Nannini   Benetton-Ford V8 B189   3

E. Pirro   Benetton-Ford DFR B188   11

30 Jul   GERMAN GP, Hockenheim

A. Nannini   Benetton-Ford V8 B189   R

E. Pirro   Benetton-Ford V8 B189   R

13 Aug   HUNGARIAN GP, Hungaroring

A. Nannini   Benetton-Ford V8 B189   R

E. Pirro   Benetton-Ford V8 B189   8

27 Aug   BELGIAN GP, Spa Francorchamps

A. Nannini   Benetton-Ford V8 B189   5

E. Pirro   Benetton-Ford V8 B189   10

10 Sept   ITALIAN GP, Monza

A. Nannini   Benetton-Ford V8 B189   R

E. Pirro   Benetton-Ford V8 B189   R

24 Sep   PORTUGUESE GP, Estoril

A. Nannini   Benetton-Ford V8 B189   4

E. Pirro   Benetton-Ford V8 B189   R

1 Oct   SPANISH GP, Jerez

A. Nannini   Benetton-Ford V8 B189   R

E. Pirro   Benetton-Ford V8 B189   R

22 Oct   JAPANESE GP, Suzuka

A. Nannini   Benetton-Ford V8 B189   1

E. Pirro   Benetton-Ford V8 B189   R

5 Nov   AUSTRALIAN GP, Adelaide

A. Nannini   Benetton-Ford V8 B189   2

E. Pirro   Benetton-Ford V8 B189   5

1990

11 Mar   UNITED STATES GP, Phoenix

A. Nannini   Benetton-Ford V8 B189B   11

N. Piquet   Benetton-Ford V8 B189B   4

25 Mar   BRAZILIAN GP, Interlagos

A. Nannini   Benetton-Ford V8 B189B   10

N. Piquet   Benetton-Ford V8 B189B   6

13 May   SAN MARINO GP, Imola

A. Nannini   Benetton-Ford V8 B190   3

N. Piquet   Benetton-Ford V8 B190   5

27 May   MONACO GP, Monte Carlo

A. Nannini   Benetton-Ford V8 B190   R

N. Piquet   Benetton-Ford V8 B190   D

10 Jun   CANADIAN GP, Montreal

A. Nannini   Benetton-Ford V8 B190   R

N. Piquet   Benetton-Ford V8 B190   2

24 Jun   MEXICAN GP, Mexico City

A. Nannini   Benetton-Ford V8 B190   4

N. Piquet   Benetton-Ford V8 B190   6

8 Jul   FRENCH GP, Paul Ricard

A. Nannini   Benetton-Ford V8 B190   16

N. Piquet   Benetton-Ford V8 B190   4

15 Jul   BRITISH GP, Silverstone

A. Nannini   Benetton-Ford V8 B190   R

N. Piquet   Benetton-Ford V8 B190   5

29 Jul   GERMAN GP, Hockenheim

A. Nannini   Benetton-Ford V8 B190   2

N. Piquet   Benetton-Ford V8 B190   R

12 Aug   HUNGARIAN GP, Hungaroring

A. Nannini   Benetton-Ford V8 B190   R

N. Piquet   Benetton-Ford V8 B190   3

26 Aug   BELGIAN GP, Spa Francorchamps

A. Nannini   Benetton-Ford V8 B190   4

N. Piquet   Benetton-Ford V8 B190   5

9 Sep   ITALIAN GP, Monza

A. Nannini   Benetton-Ford V8 B190   8

N. Piquet   Benetton-Ford V8 B190   7

23 Sep   PORTUGUESE GP, Estoril

A. Nannini   Benetton-Ford V8 B190   6

N. Piquet   Benetton-Ford V8 B190   5

30 Sep   SPANISH GP, Jerez

A. Nannini   Benetton-Ford V8 B190   3

N. Piquet   Benetton-Ford V8 B190   R

21 Oct   JAPANESE GP, Suzuka

R. Moreno   Benetton-Ford V8 B190   2

N. Piquet   Benetton-Ford V8 B190   1

4 Nov   AUSTRALIAN GP, Adelaide

R. Moreno   Benetton-Ford V8 B190   7

N. Piquet   Benetton-Ford V8 B190   1

1991

10 Mar   UNITED STATES GP, Phoenix

R. Moreno   Benetton-Ford HB B190B   R

N. Piquet   Benetton-Ford HB B190B   3

24 Mar   BRAZILIAN GP, Interlagos
R. Moreno   Benetton-Ford HB B190B   7
N. Piquet   Benetton-Ford HB B190B   5
28 Apr   SAN MARINO GP, Imola
R. Moreno   Benetton-Ford HB B191   13
N. Piquet   Benetton-Ford HB B191   R
12 May   MONACO GP, Monte Carlo
R. Moreno   Benetton-Ford HB B191   4
N. Piquet   Benetton-Ford HB B191   R
2 Jun   CANADIAN GP, Montreal
R. Moreno   Benetton-Ford HB B191   R
N. Piquet   Benetton-Ford HB B191   1
16 Jun   MEXICAN GP, Mexico City
R. Moreno   Benetton-Ford HB B191   5
N. Piquet   Benetton-Ford HB B191   R
7 Jul   FRENCH GP, Magny-Cours
R. Moreno   Benetton-Ford HB B191   R
N. Piquet   Benetton-Ford HB B191   8
14 Jul   BRITISH GP, Silverstone
R. Moreno   Benetton-Ford HB B191   R
N. Piquet   Benetton-Ford HB B191   5
28 Jul   GERMAN GP, Hockenheim
R. Moreno   Benetton-Ford HB B191   8
N. Piquet   Benetton-Ford HB B191   R
11 Aug   HUNGARIAN GP, Hungaroring
R. Moreno   Benetton-Ford HB B191   8
N. Piquet   Benetton-Ford HB B191   R
25 Aug   BELGIAN GP, Spa Francorchamps
R. Moreno   Benetton-Ford HB B191   4
N. Piquet   Benetton-Ford HB B191   3
8 Sep   ITALIAN GP, Monza
Schumacher   Benetton-Ford HB B191   5
N. Piquet   Benetton-Ford HB B191   6
22 Sep   PORTUGUESE GP, Estoril
Schumacher   Benetton-Ford HB B191   6
N. Piquet   Benetton-Ford HB B191   5
29 Sep   SPANISH GP, Montmelo
Schumacher   Benetton-Ford HB B191   6
N. Piquet   Benetton-Ford HB B191   11
20 Oct   JAPANESE GP, Suzuka
Schumacher   Benetton-Ford HB B191   R
N. Piquet   Benetton-Ford HB B191   7
3 Nov   AUSTRALIAN GP, Adelaide
Schumacher   Benetton-Ford HB B191   R
N. Piquet   Benetton-Ford HB B191   4

1992

1 Mar   SOUTH AFRICAN GP, Kyalami
Schumacher   Benetton-Ford HB B191B   4
M. Brundle   Benetton-Ford HB B191B   R
22 Mar   MEXICAN GP, Mexico City
Schumacher   Benetton-Ford HB B191B   3
M. Brundle   Benetton-Ford HB B191B   R
5 Apr   BRAZILIAN GP, Interlagos
Schumacher   Benetton-Ford HB B191B   3
M. Brundle   Benetton-Ford HB B191B   R
3 May   SPANISH GP, Montmelo
Schumacher   Benetton-Ford HB B192   2
M. Brundle   Benetton-Ford HB B192   R
17 May   SAN MARINO GP, Imola
Schumacher   Benetton-Ford HB B192   R
M. Brundle   Benetton-Ford HB B192   4
31 May   MONACO GP, Monte Carlo
Schumacher   Benetton-Ford HB B192   4
M. Brundle   Benetton-Ford HB B192   5
14 June CANADIAN GP, Montreal
Schumacher   Benetton-Ford HB B192   2
M. Brundle   Benetton-Ford HB B192   R
5 Jul   FRENCH GP, Magny-Cours
Schumacher   Benetton-Ford HB B192   R
M. Brundle   Benetton-Ford HB B192   3
12 Jul   BRITISH GP, Silverstone
Schumacher   Benetton-Ford HB B192   4
M. Brundle   Benetton-Ford HB B192   3
26 Jul   GERMAN GP, Hockenheim
Schumacher   Benetton-Ford HB B192   3
M. Brundle   Benetton-Ford HB B192   4
16 Aug   HUNGARIAN GP, Hungaroring
Schumacher   Benetton-Ford HB B192   R
M. Brundle   Benetton-Ford HB B192   5
30 Aug   BELGIAN GP, Spa Francorchamps
Schumacher   Benetton-Ford HB B192   1
M. Brundle   Benetton-Ford HB B192   4
13 Sep   ITALIAN GP, Monza
Schumacher   Benetton-Ford HB B192   3
M. Brundle   Benetton-Ford HB B192   2
27 Sep   PORTUGUESE GP, Estoril
Schumacher   Benetton-Ford HB B192   7
M. Brundle   Benetton-Ford HB B192   4

25 Oct   JAPANESE GP, Suzuka
  Schumacher   Benetton-Ford HB B192   R
  M. Brundle   Benetton-Ford HB B192   3
8 Nov   AUSTRALIAN GP, Adelaide
  Schumacher   Benetton-Ford HB B192   2
  M. Brundle   Benetton-Ford HB B192   3

1993

14 Mar   SOUTH AFRICAN GP, Kyalami
  Schumacher   Benetton-Ford HB B192B   R
  R. Patrese   Benetton-Ford HB B192B   R
28 Mar   BRAZILAN GP, Interlagos
  Schumacher   Benetton-Ford HB B192B   3
  R. Patrese   Benetton-Ford HB B192B   R
11 Apr   EUROPEAN GP, Donington Park
  Schumacher   Benetton-Ford HB B193B   R
  R. Patrese   Benetton-Ford HB B193B   5
25 Apr   SAN MARINO GP, Imola
  Schumacher   Benetton-Ford HB B193B   2
  R. Patrese   Benetton-Ford HB B193B   R
9 May   SPANISH GP, Montmelo
  Schumacher   Benetton-Ford HB B193B   3
  R. Patrese   Benetton-Ford HB B193B   4
23 May   MONACO GP, Monte Carlo
  Schumacher   Benetton-Ford HB B193B   R
  R. Patrese   Benetton-Ford HB B193B   R
13 Jun   CANADIAN GP, Montreal
  Schumacher   Benetton-Ford HB B193B   2
  R. Patrese   Benetton-Ford HB B193B   R
4 July   FRENCH GP, Magny-Cours
  Schumacher   Benetton-Ford HB B193B   3
  R. Patrese   Benetton-Ford HB B193B   10
11 Jul   BRITISH GP, Silverstone
  Schumacher   Benetton-Ford HB B193B   2
  R. Patrese   Benetton-Ford HB B193B   3
25 Jul   GERMAN GP, Hockenheim
  Schumacher   Benetton-Ford HB B193B   2
  R. Patrese   Benetton-Ford HB B193B   5
15 Aug   HUNGARIAN GP, Hungaroring
  Schumacher   Benetton-Ford HB B193B   R
  R. Patrese   Benetton-Ford HB B193B   2
29 Aug   BELGIAN GP, Spa Francorchamps
  Schumacher   Benetton-Ford HB B193B   2
  R. Patrese   Benetton-Ford HB B193B   6

12 Sep   ITALIAN GP, Monza
  Schumacher   Benetton-Ford HB B193B   R
  R. Patrese   Benetton-Ford HB B193B   5
26 Sep   PORTUGUESE GP, Estoril
  Schumacher   Benetton-Ford HB B193B   1
  R. Patrese   Benetton-Ford HB B193B   16
24 Oct   JAPANESE GP, Suzuka
  Schumacher   Benetton-Ford HB B193B   R
  R. Patrese   Benetton-Ford HB B193B   R
7 Nov   AUSTRALIAN GP, Adelaide
  Schumacher   Benetton-Ford HB B193B   R
  R. Patrese   Benetton-Ford HB B193B   8

1994

27 Mar   BRAZILIAN GP, Interlagos
  Schumacher   Benetton-Ford Z-R V8 B194   1
  J. Verstappen Benetton-Ford Z-R V8 B194   R
17 Apr   PACIFIC GP, Aida
  Schumacher   Benetton-Ford Z-R V8 B194   1
  J. Verstappen Benetton-Ford Z-R V8 B194   R
1 May   SAN MARINO GP, Imola
  Schumacher   Benetton-Ford Z-R V8 B194   1
  J. J. Lehto   Benetton-Ford Z-R V8 B194   R
15 May   MONACO GP, Monte Carlo
  Schumacher   Benetton-Ford Z-R V8 B194   1
  J. J. Lehto   Benetton-Ford Z-R V8 B194   7
29 May   SPANISH GP, Montmelo
  Schumacher   Benetton-Ford Z-R V8 B194   2
  J. J. Lehto   Benetton-Ford Z-R V8 B194   R
12 Jun   CANADIAN GP, Montreal
  Schumacher   Benetton-Ford Z-R V8 B194   1
  J. J. Lehto   Benetton-Ford Z-R V8 B194   6
3 Jul   FRENCH GP, Magny-Cours
  Schumacher   Benetton-Ford Z-R V8 B194   1
  J. Verstappen Benetton-Ford Z-R V8 B194   R
10 Jul   BRITISH GP, Silverstone
  Schumacher   Benetton-Ford Z-R V8 B194   D
  J. Verstappen Benetton-Ford Z-R V8 B194   8
31 Jul   GERMAN GP, Hockenheim
  Schumacher   Benetton-Ford Z-R V8 B194   R
  J. Verstappen Benetton-Ford Z-R V8 B194   R
14 Aug   HUNGARIAN GP, Hungaroring
  Schumacher   Benetton-Ford Z-R V8 B194   1
  J. Verstappen Benetton-Ford Z-R V8 B194   3

28 Aug   BELGIAN GP, Spa Francorchamps
Schumacher   Benetton-Ford Z-R V8 B194   D
J. Verstappen   Benetton-Ford Z-R V8 B194   3
11 Sep   ITALIAN GP, Monza
J. J. Lehto   Benetton-Ford Z-R V8 B194   9
J. Verstappen   Benetton-Ford Z-R V8 B194   R
25 Sep   PORTUGUESE GP, Estoril
J. J. Lehto   Benetton-Ford Z-R V8 B194   R
J. Verstappen   Benetton-Ford Z-R V8 B194   5
16 Oct   EUROPEAN GP, Jerez
Schumacher   Benetton-Ford Z-R V8 B194   1
J. Verstappen   Benetton-Ford Z-R V8 B194   R
6 Nov   JAPANESE GP, Suzuka
Schumacher   Benetton-Ford Z-R V8 B194   2
J. Herbert   Benetton-Ford Z-R V8 B194   R
13 Nov   AUSTRALIAN GP, Adelaide
Schumacher   Benetton-Ford Z-R V8 B194   R
J. Herbert   Benetton-Ford Z-R V8 B194   R

1995

26 Mar   BRAZILIAN GP, Interlagos
Schumacher   Benetton-Renault V10 B195   1
J. Herbert   Benetton-Renault V10 B195   R
9 April   ARGENTINE GP, Buenos Aires
Schumacher   Benetton-Renault V10 B195   3
J. Herbert   Benetton-Renault V10 B195   4
30 Apr   SAN MARINO GP, Imola
Schumacher   Benetton-Renault V10 B195   R
J. Herbert   Benetton-Renault V10 B195   7
14 May   SPANISH GP, Montmelo
Schumacher   Benetton-Renault V10 B195   1
J. Herbert   Benetton-Renault V10 B195   2
28 May   MONACO GP, Monte Carlo
Schumacher   Benetton-Renault V10 B195   1
J. Herbert   Benetton-Renault V10 B195   4
11 Jun   CANADIAN GP, Montreal
Schumacher   Benetton-Renault V10 B195   5
J. Herbert   Benetton-Renault V10 B195   R
2 Jul   FRENCH GP, Magny-Cours
Schumacher   Benetton-Renault V10 B195   1
J. Herbert   Benetton-Renault V10 B195   R
16 Jul   BRITISH GP, Silverstone
Schumacher   Benetton-Renault V10 B195   R
J. Herbert   Benetton-Renault V10 B195   1

30 Jul   GERMAN GP, Hockenheim
Schumacher   Benetton-Renault V10 B195   1
J. Herbert   Benetton-Renault V10 B195   4
13 Aug   HUNGARIAN GP, Hungaroring
Schumacher   Benetton-Renault V10 B195 11
J. Herbert   Benetton-Renault V10 B195   4
27 Aug   BELGIAN GP, Spa Francorchamps
Schumacher   Benetton-Renault V10 B195   1
J. Herbert   Benetton-Renault V10 B195   7
10 Sep   ITALIAN GP, Monza
Schumacher   Benetton-Renault V10 B195   R
J. Herbert   Benetton-Renault V10 B195   1
24 Sep   PORTUGUESE GP, Estoril
Schumacher   Benetton-Renault V10 B195   2
J. Herbert   Benetton-Renault V10 B195   7
1 Oct   EUROPEAN GP, Nurburgring
Schumacher   Benetton-Renault V10 B195   1
J. Herbert   Benetton-Renault V10 B195   5
22 Oct   PACIFIC GP, Aida
Schumacher   Benetton-Renault V10 B195   1
J. Herbert   Benetton-Renault V10 B195   6
29 Oct   JAPANESE GP, Suzuka
Schumacher   Benetton-Renault V10 B195   1
J. Herbert   Benetton-Renault V10 B195   3
12 Nov   AUSTRALIAN GP, Adelaide
Schumacher   Benetton-Renault V10 B195   R
J. Herbert   Benetton-Renault V10 B195   R

1996

10 Mar   AUSTRALIAN GP, Melbourne
J. Alesi   Benetton-Renault V10 B196   R
G. Berger   Benetton-Renault V10 B196   4
31 Mar   BRAZILIAN GP, Interlagos
J. Alesi   Benetton-Renault V10 B196   2
G. Berger   Benetton-Renault V10 B196   R
7 Apr   ARGENTINE GP, Buenos Aires
J. Alesi   Benetton-Renault V10 B196   3
G. Berger   Benetton-Renault V10 B196   R
28 Apr   EUROPEAN GP, Nurburgring
J. Alesi   Benetton-Renault V10 B196   R
G. Berger   Benetton-Renault V10 B196   9
5 May   SAN MARINO GP, Imola
J. Alesi   Benetton-Renault V10 B196   6
G. Berger   Benetton-Renault V10 B196   3

19 May   MONACO GP, Monte Carlo
  J. Alesi   Benetton-Renault V10 B196 R
  G. Berger   Benetton-Renault V10 B196 R
2 Jun   SPANISH GP, Montmelo
  J. Alesi   Benetton-Renault V10 B196 2
  G. Berger   Benetton-Renault V10 B196 R
16 Jun   CANADIAN GP, Montreal
  J. Alesi   Benetton-Renault V10 B196 3
  G. Berger   Benetton-Renault V10 B196 R
30 June FRENCH GP, Magny-Cours
  J. Alesi   Benetton-Renault V10 B196 3
  G. Berger   Benetton-Renault V10 B196 4
14 Jul   BRITISH GP, Silverstone
  J. Alesi   Benetton-Renault V10 B196 R
  G. Berger   Benetton-Renault V10 B196 2
28 Jul   GERMAN GP, Hockenheim
  J. Alesi   Benetton-Renault V10 B196 2
  G. Berger   Benetton-Renault V10 B196 13
11 Aug   HUNGARIAN GP, Hungaroring
  J. Alesi   Benetton-Renault V10 B196 3
  G. Berger   Benetton-Renault V10 B196 R
25 Aug   BELGIAN GP, Spa Francorchamps
  J. Alesi   Benetton-Renault V10 B196 4
  G. Berger   Benetton-Renault V10 B196 6
8 Sep   ITALIAN GP, Monza
  J. Alesi   Benetton-Renault V10 B196 2
  G. Berger   Benetton-Renault V10 B196 R
22 Sep   PORTUGUESE GP, Estoril
  J. Alesi   Benetton-Renault V10 B196 4
  G. Berger   Benetton-Renault V10 B196 6
13 Oct   JAPANESE GP, Suzuka
  J. Alesi   Benetton-Renault V10 B196 R
  G. Berger   Benetton-Renault V10 B196 4

1997

9 Mar   AUSTRALIAN GP, Melbourne
  J. Alesi   Benetton-Renault V10 B197 R
  G. Berger   Benetton-Renault V10 B197 4
30 Mar   BRAZILIAN GP, Interlagos
  J. Alesi   Benetton-Renault V10 B197 6
  G. Berger   Benetton-Renault V10 B197 2
13 Apr   ARGENTINE GP, Buenos Aires
  J. Alesi   Benetton-Renault V10 B197 7
  G. Berger   Benetton-Renault V10 B197 6

27 Apr   SAN MARINO GP, Imola
  J. Alesi   Benetton-Renault V10 B197 5
  G. Berger   Benetton-Renault V10 B197 R
11 May   MONACO GP, Monte Carlo
  J. Alesi   Benetton-Renault V10 B197 R
  G. Berger   Benetton-Renault V10 B197 9
25 May   SPANISH GP, Montmelo
  J. Alesi   Benetton-Renault V10 B197 3
  G. Berger   Benetton-Renault V10 B197 10
15 Jun   CANADIAN GP, Montreal
  J. Alesi   Benetton-Renault V10 B197 2
  A. Wurz   Benetton-Renault V10 B197 R
29 Jun   FRENCH GP, Magny-Cours
  J. Alesi   Benetton-Renault V10 B197 5
  A. Wurz   Benetton-Renault V10 B197 R
13 Jul   BRITISH GP, Silverstone
  J. Alesi   Benetton-Renault V10 B197 2
  A. Wurz   Benetton-Renault V10 B197 3
27 Jul   GERMAN GP, Hockenheim
  J. Alesi   Benetton-Renault V10 B197 6
  G. Berger   Benetton-Renault V10 B197 1
10 Aug   HUNGARIAN GP, Hungaroring
  J. Alesi   Benetton-Renault V10 B197 11
  G. Berger   Benetton-Renault V10 B197 8
24 Aug   BELGIAN GP, Spa Francorchamps
  J. Alesi   Benetton-Renault V10 B197 8
  G. Berger   Benetton-Renault V10 B197 6
7 Sep   ITALIAN GP, Monza
  J. Alesi   Benetton-Renault V10 B197 2
  G. Berger   Benetton-Renault V10 B197 7
21 Sep   AUSTRIAN GP, A1-Ring
  J. Alesi   Benetton-Renault V10 B197 R
  G. Berger   Benetton-Renault V10 B197 10
28 Sep   LUXEMBOURG GP, Nurburgring
  J. Alesi   Benetton-Renault V10 B197 2
  G. Berger   Benetton-Renault V10 B197 4
12 Oct   JAPANESE GP, Suzuka
  J. Alesi   Benetton-Renault V10 B197 5
  G. Berger   Benetton-Renault V10 B197 8
26 Oct   EUROPEAN GP, Jerez
  J. Alesi   Benetton-Renault V10 B197 13
  G. Berger   Benetton-Renault V10 B197 4

1998

8 Mar	AUSTRALIAN GP, Melbourne	
G. Fisichella	Benetton-Playlife B198	R
A. Wurz	Benetton-Playlife B198	7
29 Mar	BRAZILIAN GP, Interlagos	
G. Fisichella	Benetton-Playlife B198	6
A. Wurz	Benetton-Playlife B198	4
12 Apr	ARGENTINE GP, Buenos Aires	
G. Fisichella	Benetton-Playlife B198	7
A. Wurz	Benetton-Playlife B198	4
26 Apr	SAN MARINO GP, Imola	
G. Fisichella	Benetton-Playlife B198	R
A. Wurz	Benetton-Playlife B198	R
10 May	SPANISH GP, Barcelona	
G. Fisichella	Benetton-Playlife B198	R
A. Wurz	Benetton-Playlife B198	4
24 May	MONACO GP, Monte Carlo	
G. Fisichella	Benetton-Playlife B198	2
A. Wurz	Benetton-Playlife B198	R
7 Jun	CANADIAN GP, Montreal	
G. Fisichella	Benetton-Playlife B198	2
A. Wurz	Benetton-Playlife B198	4
28 Jun	FRENCH GP, Magny-Cours	
G. Fisichella	Benetton-Playlife B198	9
A. Wurz	Benetton-Playlife B198	5
12 Jul	BRITISH GP, Silverstone	
G. Fisichella	Benetton-Playlife B198	5
A. Wurz	Benetton-Playlife B198	4
26 Jul	AUSTRIAN GP, A1-Ring	
G. Fisichella	Benetton-Playlife B198	R
A. Wurz	Benetton-Playlife B198	9
2 Aug	GERMAN GP, Hockenheim	
G. Fisichella	Benetton-Playlife B198	7
A. Wurz	Benetton-Playlife B198	11
16 Aug	HUNGARIAN GP, Hungaroring	
G. Fisichella	Benetton-Playlife B198	8
A. Wurz	Benetton-Playlife B198	R
30 Aug	BELGIAN GP, Spa-Francorchamps	
G. Fisichella	Benetton-Playlife B198	R
A. Wurz	Benetton-Playlife B198	R
13 Sep	ITALIAN GP, Monza	
G. Fisichella	Benetton-Playlife B198	8
A. Wurz	Benetton-Playlife B198	R
29 Sep	LUXEMBOURG GP, Nurburgring	
G. Fisichella	Benetton-Playlife B198	6
A. Wurz	Benetton-Playlife B198	7
1 Nov	JAPANESE GP, Suzuka	
G. Fisichella	Benetton-Playlife B198	8
A. Wurz	Benetton-Playlife B198	9

Appendix 2

Benetton – team statistics

GP RECORD TO END OF 1998:
(From 1981 including cars
under Toleman name)

Grands Prix contested:	267
Pole positions:	16
Victories:	27
Fastest race laps:	37

GP CONSTRUCTORS'
CHAMPIONSHIP PLACINGS:

Toleman

Year		Place	Points
1981	–	–	no points
1982	–	–	no points
1983	–	9th	10 points
1984	–	7th	16 points
1985	–	–	no points

Benetton

Year		Place	Points
1986	–	6th	19 points
1987	–	5th	28 points
1988	–	3rd	39 points
1989	–	4th	39 points
1990	–	3rd	71 points
1991	–	4th	38.5 points
1992	–	3rd	91 points
1993	–	3rd	72 points
1994	–	2nd	103 points
1995	–	1st	137 points
1996	–	3rd	68 points
1997	–	3rd	67 points
1998	–	5th	33 points

Appendix 3

Benetton – most successful drivers

MICHAEL SCHUMACHER (D). Born 3.1.69. F1 debut, 1991, Belgium (Jordan). Drove for Benetton 1991–95. 33 wins, 19 with Benetton. World Champion 1994 and 1995 driving for Benetton.

GERHARD BERGER (A) Born 27.8.59. F1 debut, 1984, Austria (ATS). Drove for Benetton 1986 and 1996–97. 10 wins, two with Benetton.

NELSON PIQUET (BR) Born 17.8.52. F1 debut, 1978, Germany (Ensign). Drove for Benetton 1990–91. 23 wins, three with Benetton. World Champion 1981 and 1983 (with Brabham) and 1987 (with Williams).

ALESSANDRO NANNINI (I) Born 7.7.59. F1 debut, 1986, Brazil (Minardi). Drove for Benetton 1988–90 when F1 career prematurely ended by arm injuries sustained in helicopter accident. One win, with Benetton.

JEAN ALESI (F). Born 11.6.64. F1 debut, 1989, France (Tyrrell). Drove for Benetton 1996–97. One win, with Ferrari. Best Benetton results, second in Brazil, Spain, Germany and Italy (1996) plus Canada, Britain, Italy and Luxembourg (1997).

JOHNNY HERBERT (GB). Born 25.6.64. F1 debut, 1989, Brazil (Benetton). Drove for Benetton 1989 and 1994–95. Two wins, both with Benetton.

GIANCARLO FISICHELLA (I). Born 14.1.73. F1 debut, 1996, Australia (Minardi). Drove for Benetton 1998. Best Benetton results, second in Monaco and Canada plus pole position Austria (1998).

ALEXANDER WURZ (A). Born 15.2.74. F1 debut, 1997, Canada (Benetton). Drove for Benetton 1997 and 1998. Best Benetton results third in Britain (1997), fourth in Brazil, Argentina, Spain, Canada and Britain (1998).

OTHER BOOKS OF INTEREST

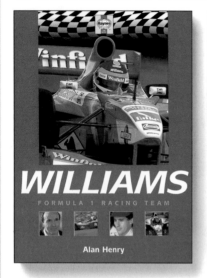

WILLIAMS
FORMULA 1 RACING TEAM

Alan Henry

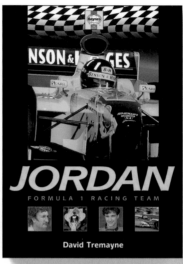

JORDAN
FORMULA 1 RACING TEAM

David Tremayne

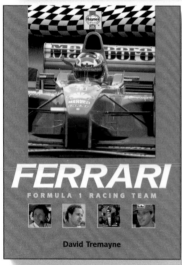

FERRARI
FORMULA 1 RACING TEAM

David Tremayne

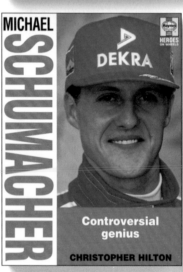

MICHAEL **SCHUMACHER**

HEROES ON WHEELS

Controversial genius

CHRISTOPHER HILTON

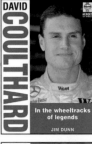

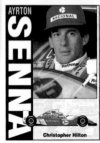

AUDIO CASSETTES A collection of audio cassettes featuring top Formula 1 drivers is available from **Audiosport Ltd**, The Fairway, Bush Fair, Harlow, Essex CM18 6LY (tel: 01279 444707). Scripted by Christopher Hilton and narrated by Julian Harries, the Grand Prix Heroes series includes cassettes on Jacques Villeneuve, Michael Schumacher, Mika Hakkinen and Johnny Herbert.

For more information on books please contact: Customer Services, Haynes Publishing, Sparkford, Nr Yeovil, Somerset BA22 7JJ
Tel. 01963 440635 **Fax:** 01963 440001
Int. tel: +44 1963 440635 **Fax:** +44 1963 440001
E-mail: sales@haynes-manuals.co.uk **Web site:** http://www.haynes.com

Haynes
THE BOOK